The Gospel according to Ruth

Devotional studies in the book of Ruth

Iain D Campbell

DayOne

For Iain, Stephen and Emily
with the hope and prayer
that they too will make the choice Ruth made.

© Day One Publications 2003
First printed 2003

ISBN 1 903087 36-8

9 781903 087367

All Scripture quotations are from The New King James Version
©Thomas Nelson Inc. except where marked NLT, New Living Translation, © .
British Library Cataloguing in Publication Data available

Published by Day One Publications
3 Epsom Business Park, Kiln Lane, Epsom, Surrey KT17 1JF.
01372 728 300 FAX 01372 722 400
email—sales@dayone.co.uk
web site—www.dayone.co.uk
North American—e-mail-sales@dayonebookstore.com
North American web site—www.dayonebookstore.com

Designed by Steve Devane and printed by CPD

COVER: ARON BURTON / STEVE DEVANE

Contents

Foreword

The following devotional studies in the Book of Ruth were first delivered as a series of sermons in Back Free Church of Scotland, Isle of Lewis, between September and December 1996. I am grateful to Back Free Church Tape Ministry for financing the transcription of these sermons, and encouraging their publication. I am also grateful to Sarah Gillbe for the work of transcribing. In editing the text for publication, I have taken Scripture quotations from the New King James Version, except occasionally when I have preferred the more colloquial New Living Translation (NLT). I would like to thank Day One Publications for considering this manuscript for publication, and for all the editorial help received. Above all, to Anne my own 'Ruth', I would like, once again to express my love and affection. Like Leah, Rachel and Ruth in their own homes, she has been the pillar of ours.

Iain D. Campbell
January 2003

The Book of Ruth is, at heart, a romance. It is a book about love which reflects the theme of the Bible, because the Bible too is a book about love. The unifying message of the Scriptures is that God is love, and that God has loved—loved with such intensity and depth that he gave his Son to die for a lost, sinful and unlovely world. Perhaps that is why Martin Luther said that the Bible could be read in miniature in John 3:16—the great statement that God loved the world to such an extent that he gave his only-begotten son, that whoever believes in him should not perish but have everlasting life.

The Old Testament tells us of how God prepared the world for the coming of the Messiah, the Lord Jesus Christ. His life, death and resurrection were explained both by Jesus himself and by the apostles in Old Testament terms, and with Old Testament motifs. It is possible to begin with the Books of Moses, and to work through the prophetic literature and the rest of the Old Testament writings, and to find Christ there (cf. Luke 24:27; John 5:39).

Part of the reason for this study is to show that the story of Ruth, written as one of the historical books of the Old Testament, bears witness to the love of God which ultimately would show itself in the coming of Jesus Christ, the Son of David. Indeed, the Book of Ruth teaches us not only that God loves a lost and sinful world, but that he opens up doors of remarkable blessing through his redemptive love. It is a theme that is consonant with the whole message of the Old and New Testaments.

In fact, it is interesting that the three great love passages of the Old Testament—the story of Rebekah, who became the wife of Isaac (Genesis 24), Ruth who became the wife of Boaz, and the 'Shulammite' who became the wife of Solomon—are all related to the revelation of God's gracious saving covenant at different points of Old Testament history. God, in other words, illustrates his covenant love for us in these stories which unite in their themes of love and marriage.

After the destruction of the world with a flood, God made covenantal promises to Noah. He had saved the family of Noah, thereby showing that families were to be integral to the saving purposes of his grace. One of the covenant promises God made was that the Japhethites (the Gentiles, who were strangers to the covenant line, or seed) would dwell in the tents of

Shem (Genesis 9:27). In other words, it was God's immediate purpose in the Old Testament to reveal his covenant redemption to the Semitic, Jewish line; but it was his ultimate purpose in the world to extend the blessings of that covenant to those who ordinarily had no claim to the promises and privileges of the covenant of God's grace.

The covenant was ratified with Abraham, to whom God promised that in him all the nations of the world would receive blessing (Genesis 12:1–3; 17:7–8). The favours of God's covenanted redemption would extend to all ends of the earth by sinners being brought in to the covenant family. The Old Testament thus plays on an immediate/ultimate theme: the Jewish people, in the first instance, are those to whom the redemptive purposes and promises are given, with the end in view that the blessing of Abraham will extend to the Gentiles through Jesus Christ (cf. Galatians 3:13). It is this covenantal theme that unifies the Bible, and emphasises for us that although it is a book of sixty-six books, it is a book of one message.

The covenant of God's grace was revealed to and ratified with Abraham, Moses and David. In each case it is exemplified, applied and illustrated by the theme of love and marriage. Following God's covenant with Abraham ('the covenant of circumcision' according to Acts 7:8), we find Abraham sending his servant to Mesopotamia to find a wife for his son, Isaac (Genesis 24). It is surely significant that the longest chapter of Genesis is reserved for what has been called 'the greatest love story ever told'. Abraham is the father of Isaac, the son of his old age, and of the promise God made with him. Ultimately, as the New Testament argues, the focus of this promise is Jesus Christ (Galatians 3:16). The immediate focus is on Isaac, however, and God's redemptive intention is both illustrated and ratified by the bringing of Rebekah into the line of God's saving and redemptive purpose. She is domesticated in the line of Abraham, and becomes the mother of Jacob, through whom God will continue to reveal his saving purpose to the world.

The Book of Ruth is also a great love story with a similar theme. It is contextualised within the Mosaic covenant, written against the backdrop of the law code which God gave to his people. The law revealed to them the nature of sin against God, and acted like a fence within which God's covenant people might enjoy the blessings of that covenant. In the case of

Ruth, the law highlighted the fact that, as a Moabitess, she was naturally excluded from the fellowship of God and the blessings of his covenant. However, the same law which revealed her natural alienation from God also made provision for her, as a widow and stranger, to enter into the covenant community of God's people. Her entrance into that new fellowship is sealed by her marriage to Boaz, and is another example of God bringing those who are outside the covenant into that very covenant.

In 2 Samuel 7, God further sealed his covenant redemption by making specific promises to David. These promises focus our attention on the Davidic line, from which the Messiah would come. It is not insignificant that the New Testament should open with a statement of Christ's descent from David (Matthew 1:1ff); nor is it insignificant that it should close with an affirmation that Christ is the root and offspring of David (Revelation 22:16).

The promise that David would have a son who would sit on his throne was fulfilled immediately in Solomon, but ultimately in Christ, the 'greater than Solomon'. The Song of Solomon, a powerful poetic celebration of the marriage of Solomon, is at one level the greatest celebration of human love which we find in the Old Testament. However, at a deeper level, it is a climactic revelation of the message which the Old Testament preaches in preparation for the coming of Jesus Christ: that God extends the blessings of the (Davidic) covenant to those who are outside by bringing them into that covenant.

Thus the marriages of Rebekah to Isaac, of Ruth to Boaz and of the 'Shulammite' to Solomon, all illustrate the essence of the Gospel: that Jesus Christ, the Mediator of God's covenant, came to extend the blessings of Abraham to those who were 'without God and without hope', who were by nature the children of wrath, who were 'aliens from the commonwealth of Israel and strangers to the covenants of promise' (Ephesians 2:12). This he did by bringing sinners, who are alienated and distanced from the mercy and grace of God, into a covenantal marriage union with himself. The story of Rebekah, of Ruth and of the Shulammite, find their ultimate meaning and fulfilment in the Book of Revelation, when God says to us 'Come, I will show you the bride—the Lamb's wife' (Revelation 21:9).

Thus while the narrative of the Book of Ruth is full of interest as a

Introduction

powerful story of choice, of love, and of blessing, its deeper meaning is to be found at the level of what biblical scholars call the 'metanarrative'—the big story—of the Bible. For at last, there is only one Gospel, and one covenant of grace, and sinners are saved because God is still looking for a wife for Abraham's great Son, the Lord Jesus. They are saved because the law has made provision for redemption through kinship, and there is one whose work is sufficient to bring us into the bond of the covenant. They are saved because David's greater Son, the Lord Jesus Christ, loved his church and gave himself for it. The love stories of the Old Testament, understood against the backdrop of the covenantal unity of the Bible, point forward to the marriage of the Lamb.

It is in this context that we must approach the story of Ruth. In the following chapters, I hope that we will uncover something of the hidden depths of meaning and significance of this great book of the Old Testament. May the Lord open our eyes so that we will see the love of the Saviour displayed and illustrated in the story of Ruth.

The story

Boaz was the father of Obed (his mother was Ruth).
Matthew 1:5 NLT.

The short Book of Ruth appears in the Bible between the Book of Judges on the one hand, and the First Book of Samuel on the other; these are two momentous books that tell of the varied and difficult experiences of the people of God in the Old Testament. Amid that history, Ruth's story shines through the pages of the Old Testament like a light in the darkness, like a bright star in the night sky. It is one of the most moving and one of the most beautiful books of the Bible; and as we study this book of Ruth together I hope that we will see that its significance is out of all proportion to its length.

Two books in the Old Testament are named after women. One is the book of Ruth, and the other is the Book of Esther. At one level these two books tell very different stories. Esther was a queen; Ruth was a very lowly peasant girl. Esther was a Jewess who married a Gentile; Ruth was a Gentile who married a Jew. The Book of Esther opens with a feast, while the Book of Ruth opens with a famine. The Book of Esther comes to a close with the hanging of an enemy; the Book of Ruth comes to a close with the birth of a child.

Both of these books, for all of their differences, are concerned with one theme, and that is the issue of God's preserving his own people, and his own church in the world. In both cases we find the people of God in difficult circumstances, and in both cases we find God intervening to help, encourage and preserve his redeemed people.

That fact alone makes these books worth studying. There are times when we are tempted to think that the church has no future, and that the cause of the church is doomed to extinction. The detractors tell us that the work and witness of the church are no longer relevant in our so-called postmodern age, and that the church is a dying institution. So it is important to come to these great books of the Old Testament, particularly this Book of Ruth, to remind ourselves that the church is the preserve of God. God's people are under his supervision and superintendence. God has pledged himself to the maintenance of his own cause, and to the furtherance of his own Gospel. He has promised that men will be blessed in and through the saving work of Christ; the Book of Ruth serves to remind us that however low the cause of Truth might appear to be to the eyes of men, before the eyes of God it is marching forward in triumphal procession, gathering momentum and blessing and changing the lives of men and women and children along the way. The Book of Ruth reminds us that to the uttermost the God who preserves his own church and his own cause in the world will save sinners and bring them into what the prophet Ezekiel called 'the bond of his own covenant' (Ezekiel 20:37).

Ruth: An Overview

If we are to spend some time gleaning in the chapters of Ruth, then we need to understand the setting, the meaning and the themes that are covered in this great book of four chapters that we have in the Old Testament. It is important, I think, to take an overview of this great Book of Ruth, and to look at the movement of the story.

I like Warren Wiersbe's summary of the four chapters of Ruth. In his little book entitled *Put your life together: Studies in the Book of Ruth*, Wiersbe describes the first chapter of Ruth as the *weeping* chapter, the second as the *working* chapter, the third as the *waiting* chapter, and the fourth as the *wedding* chapter. Or, in other words, this is a story about the heart: a story, first, about *broken* hearts; second, about *comforted* hearts; third, about *assured* hearts; and fourth, about *joyful* hearts.

The first chapter of the Book of Ruth, is the chapter of the broken heart: it's a *weeping* chapter. It tells a story of sorrow. Naomi weeps. Orpah weeps. Ruth weeps.

Then we come into Chapter Two, the great *working* chapter, the chapter of the comforted heart, in which Ruth finds herself in the fields of Boaz. There, among the workers and the people of Boaz, gleaning in his fields at the beginning of Bethlehem's harvest, Ruth discovers that God has been going before her. She finds that the God of the covenant is her great comforter and provider. In the service of Boaz, Ruth experiences peace and contentment. This chapter is full of spiritual significance and full of spiritual lessons and encouragement both for Ruth and for us.

In Chapter Three we find Ruth *waiting*, and through waiting she finds assurance that Boaz will serve her in his capacity as kinsman-redeemer. She has to be patient. She has to go to a certain place at a certain time and she has to wait *for* Boaz, and she has to wait *on* Boaz and she has to wait *until* Boaz can deal with and regulate all the affairs that concern her personally now that she has come among God's people. It's a chapter full of submission in which Ruth bows before the Lord God, and finds the assurance that her heart needs.

The lesson of this third chapter is fundamental to our understanding of the story, and of the whole Gospel itself. There are many people in the world today who are waiting *for* something, in order that they will become Christians. Perhaps something major is going to intrude into their lives and improve their lot. They are waiting for some great act, some brilliant miracle, but the answer to our need is not to wait *for* something but to wait *on* someone. It is those who wait **on** the Lord that renew their strength (Isaiah 40:31); perhaps the problem for many people is that they are waiting *for* him when they should be waiting *on him*. Chapter Three of Ruth is a waiting chapter, a submission chapter in which Ruth bows before the word and the law and the claims of God as every sinner must do who will come to Christ.

Finally, Chapter Four is the great *wedding* chapter, in which hearts are filled with joy. The final consummation of God's purposes for Ruth the Moabitess is realised when she is joined in marriage to Boaz and a child is born. There, in the marriage of Ruth and Boaz there is great satisfaction, so, in the course of this narrative, we move from sorrow through service and submission to satisfaction. That is precisely the movement of the Gospel from beginning to end. The Gospel comes to us in a world of sin and of sorrow, a world of broken hearts and broken dreams and broken promises and broken lives. The Gospel is good news indeed for a world that finds us in the midst of death; sin has brought death, but grace has brought life into the experience of men and women. Only those who have embraced the Gospel can say, 'O death, where is your sting?' (1 Corinthians 15:55).

The Gospel that finds us in the midst of all this sin and sorrow and heartache brings us at last to the place of submission before Christ and satisfaction in Christ. If we have not experienced that great movement of the Grace of God in our soul then we have missed the greatest thing in the world. With all the problems and all the burdens and all the heartache of living in a sin-sick world, there is a Gospel that is able to bring the heart of man out of sorrow and into satisfaction, out of misery and into peace, out of the bondage of sin and the meaninglessness of our godless life into the fulfilment and the completion and the purpose that there is in Jesus Christ.

Until Jesus Christ fills the void in the heart of man, there will always be sorrow and heartache, there will always be meaningless and futility, and men will always waken up and say 'What is it all for?' The world will continue to deceive and delude, to promise and to renege on its promises. Without a relationship with Jesus Christ, men will chase their dreams and pursue their plans down every road and every avenue of human experience and they will always return saying, 'I did not find it there. I went down this road looking for peace and meaning and satisfaction, looking for purpose, and at the end of it there was brokenness—there were broken plans and broken dreams.' The Bible says that the man who 'sows the wind' will 'reap the whirlwind' (Hosea 8:7).

The person who tries to fill his life with something other than Christ will fail to secure the peace that he needs, but the person who has come to Christ, who has bowed before Him and who has come to see the fullness that there is in him, has found where real contentment and joy are to be found. Christians may still have burdens and heartaches and sorrow in this life; but they also experience 'the peace that passes all understanding' (Philippians 4:7). Christ is the only path that does not bring disappointment. There is one place to which poor, needy sinners can go to find real peace and rest for their souls: by taking all their sins and all their burdens to the Saviour. They have found in him a resting-place and he has made them glad.

That, after all, is the great issue of the Bible. Isaiah described the Saviour as 'the shadow of a great rock in a weary land' (Isaiah 32:2). Here is this great image of people living in the wilderness, with all its problems: the sun beating mercilessly and the drought and the dryness and the barren desert around them. All they want is shelter, a rock perhaps, which will give some shade from the sun, something to keep them and to preserve them; to take away the burning, searing heat of the sun and the dryness and the barrenness of the desert and the meaninglessness of it all. God says there is a man, the God-man, who is like a hiding place in the storm, the shadow of a great rock in our weary life. To come to him is to experience the transition from emptiness to fullness, despair to rejoicing.

That is exactly the movement and message of the Book of Ruth. It is possible for a human life to travel from sorrow to satisfaction, from tears to rejoicing, from bitterness to blessedness, from emptiness to fullness, from darkness to light, from chains and bondage and sin to liberty and freedom and covenant.

Ruth: the Times

It is important to notice the setting of the Book of Ruth. This short story is set for us very carefully and very precisely at a particular time in the Old Testament. We read in the opening verse: 'It came to pass in the days when the judges ruled'. These are words that we can read very quickly and pass them by; but they are of tremendous significance.

This opening verse does not tell us at what point in the history of the judges the Book of Ruth was set, but we know from the New Testament that Boaz, who is to feature highly in the narrative, was the son of Rahab the prostitute. She believed in God and was saved at the destruction of Jericho by Joshua when he overthrew that land (Judges 2). That, I think, hints that this story took place early on in the period of the judges.

Now if you know your Bible, you will be aware of one outstanding characteristic of this period of Old Testament history. It was something that occurred time and time again in this period and is summarised in the last verse of the Book of Judges, where we read that 'in those days there was no king in Israel. Every man did that which was right in his own eyes' (Judges 21:25).

In order to understand the Book of Ruth, we need to underline and underscore this summary of the period in which the Book of Ruth is set.

What kind of days were these, in which the judges ruled? They were days when there was no king, when there was no person occupying the throne. Instead, God sent judges to rule and to lead the people, to declare the word and will of God to the people. Through these judges God delivered his people from the hands of their enemies who were oppressing them and who were keeping them in bondage. This whole period had one great characteristic and it was that 'every man did that which was right in his own eyes'.

The problem was not that Israel had no Bible. They had the word of God in the law code of the Mosaic covenant. The whole purpose of that law was to remind them of their identity as covenant people, to regulate their behaviour as covenant people, and to open the door of blessing and fellowship with God as his covenant people. They had God's word, in written form, and that word had to do with their whole lives, their thinking and their behaviour.

The one great feature of this whole period was that Israel neither paid attention to the message or to the messengers; neither to the law nor to those who delivered it to them; everyone did what was right in his own eyes. It was an age of tremendous independence from God, manifesting a spirit of self-rule, and of self-confidence. God said one thing, but the people did another. What was written in God's law was of little consequence. God laid down standards of absolute morality and ethics, but that was of little import. Every man claimed his right to live as he claimed; men did what they wanted, and God was left out. What God said was of secondary importance and was almost irrelevant and peripheral.

However, this was not an irreligious age. There was no shortage of religion, no shortage of judges, or of messengers from God. However, when it actually came to the individual response of men and women to the claims of God's truth, every man did as he pleased. And what was true of the judges long ago is still true; indeed, the summary of Judges 21:25 could be a summary of our own generation and nation.

Today, we have far more than Israel ever had. The people of God in the Old Testament age had the written law code, as well as the great histories passed on to them by word of mouth. We, however, have a closed Bible, a full, final, completed canon of scripture; God has spoken his last word in Jesus Christ and he has recorded it for us in the pages of the Bible from beginning to end. Here is the word of God. These lively oracles of scripture, our Bible, are full of God and full of the truth of his salvation. The Bible speaks of the absolute standards that God requires, but what is the one outstanding characteristic of this generation of ours in which we live? Is it not that men and women are doing what is right in their own eyes? When we survey every stratum and every area of society we will find men and women claiming their inalienable right to do what they will with their own lives, and to do what is right in their own eyes.

Every parent knows the struggle of trying to get their children to follow a certain course of action, and being met with resistance. They say, 'I want to do this' or 'I want to do that'. One of the difficulties of parenting is to teach children that we do not have an inalienable right to do what we want with our own lives. It is this mindset that does irreparable damage to human lives, societies, and even churches. Why are there so many pulpits where doctrines are preached that are contrary to the doctrines of scripture? Why do men (and women) preach things that do not accord with the great declarations of God's final authority and revelation in the Bible? Simply because they are claiming a right to dispense with the written, authoritative, final word of God in the Scriptures.

Many of our secular colleges and universities are selling to our young people this great fundamental ethos that people can live as they please. Yet God says that is the most destructive principle by which a man can live. It will destroy a life, a society, a community, a church. Time after time, history has repeated itself at this very point. 'Every man did that which was right in his own eyes'. Every man made up the rules on the spot. Every man looked at his own situation and decided to go his own way, irrespective of what God was saying. That permissiveness is the most destructive principle in the universe.

Yet, the amazing thing is that it was 'in the days when the judges ruled' that the Book of Ruth was set. Even with all this spiritual rebellion against God, with all this anarchy and independence that was bringing society to the very brink of destruction, God was at work. He was working to draw men and women out of the destruction and the sorrow and the power of sin and to bring them into submission to himself.

This is still the case. The Gospel of God's redeeming grace is the one thing that can save this world. Even when men are lobbying for all their rights, changing the glory of the Creator for that of the creature (Romans 1:23–25), God's grace is abounding in human experience. It may have been 'the days when the judges ruled'; but that is when Ruth was saved and was brought by grace into submission to God, into the bond of the covenant. When the covenant people forfeited the blessings of the covenant, this stranger inherited them and entered into them.

Perhaps one thing that keeps some people from coming to Christ is the thought that to live as a Christian will mean to swim against the tide, to go a way that is different from the way everyone else is going. It is not easy to swim against the current of thought patterns and ethical behaviours and standards by which friends and colleagues are living by. This world, with all its patterns of rebellion and apostasy will pass away. The cost of following Christ may be great, but infinitely greater is the reward he promises to those who know him personally. If God is for us and with us, then who can be against us? Paul, that great Apostle of the Gentiles, said on one occasion, 'At my first trial, no man stood with me, not one' (2 Timothy 4:16). Paul is standing in the footsteps of his master, who stood against the stream of the world's hostility and the world's anarchy and the world's rebellion and who said 'there is no-one who acknowledges me ... no one cares for my soul' (Psalm 142:4).

It may be that for us to take up the cross and to follow Jesus Christ will be to say 'no one cares'. It may be that for you to become a Christian will mean having to say 'No man stood with me'. It is far better to be alone on the side of Christ than to drift with millions into death and destruction. 'In the days that the judges ruled' many people drifted away from God in a self-dependent, wilful, rebellious spirit. These were days of anarchy and rebellion against God. Yet God saved and brought sinners out of that darkness and into his light, and he does it still.

Ruth: the Themes

What, then, is the Book of Ruth about?

First of all it is about God's *promises*. It is a book that reminds us that once God has made a pledge, he will honour that pledge. Once God has committed himself to a particular course of action, he will carry that commitment through to the very end. What promise had he made? He had made covenant promises, covenant pledges, way back at the dawn of human history. He had committed himself to the salvation of sinners.

Adam sinned and dragged the whole of mankind with him into hopelessness and into despair and ruin, but God came to him where he was, in the darkness of his loss, and God said to him 'I will send one who will bruise the head of the serpent' (Genesis 3:15). God undertook to deliver sinners out of the grip of Satan and the fear and the bondage of death. God renewed his covenant pledge with Noah and with Abraham, with Moses and David. Down through the years of the history of the Old Testament, he revealed himself as a covenant God and Saviour, promising to bring a people out of sin's captivity and bondage into the light and the liberty of the Gospel.

Ruth is all about the fulfilment of the promises of God. One of its great themes is God's faithfullness to his pledge, to his covenant commitment. It is about his determination to save, his power to save and his ability to save. God has seen the bitterness of sin. God knows what man has done to himself, and even before the world was made, he pledged himself to the recovery of man out of sin. As the Puritan Thomas Goodwin put it, writing boldly three hundred years ago, 'the heads of the persons of the Godhead work together in order to effect a way of salvation for fallen man.' These promises of God's salvation are displayed in the Gospel. God can save! He does save, and he will save every sinner who comes to him; that is his promise.

'Those who come unto me,' he says, 'I will in no wise cast out' (John 6:37). Ruth comes in need to the God of the covenant, and he does not cast her out. The free offer of the Gospel is built upon this great divine promise. Whatever our lives are like, whatever our background, our theological hang-ups, our sin and despair, he says that there is hope for us in his covenant pledge. That is why Hugh Martin, the great Scottish theologian, described the free offer of the Gospel as a call from within the covenant. Young and old are called to come to the everlasting covenant, whose promises are made sure in the blood of Jesus Christ. Those who come to him discover that he is not a God who breaks promises, or reneges on pledges, who does not fulfil commitments.

The Book of Ruth, therefore, brings us to the very essence of the Gospel. Its background is in the covenant revelation of God's salvation, and its ultimate focus is on the Mediator who will be born from the royal line of

Chapter 1

David. Christ invites us to search the Scriptures, because they testify of him. It is in that light that we must search the Book of Ruth.

The Book of Ruth is also a story of God's *providences*. It is a story of things that God allows to come into the lives of men and women. It is a story about experiences that are hard to bear and about burdens that are difficult to carry; about heartache and loss. It is a story in which famines and feastings are interwoven. Here there is wailing and weeping mingled with wedding celebrations and joy. It reminds us of the havoc sin has wrought in the world, and that God sometimes allows the most indescribable difficulties to meet us along the way. It is a story that reminds us that he may take us to the very edge of our reason and to the very edge of despair, before we can know the liberty and the blessing of his peace. It is a story that reminds us that sometimes we have to feel the thorn on the stem before we can see the rose in its full bloom. It teaches us that although weeping endures in the night, joy will come in the morning. It reminds us that light and darkness intermingle in the experience of men and women; that God brings people through the shadows, through the fire, through the water, into the wealthy place (Psalm 66:12).

Ruth had gone through the years of idolatry in Moab, and there, around the grave of her husband and her brother-in-law and her father-in-law, she made her pledge to come to God and to bow before the covenant promises of the sovereign God of all the Earth, who does all things well. The God of Ruth is the same God still; he rules over the night as over the day, over the shadows as over the light, over death as over life. For us to know this God personally is to be able to say, 'we know that all things work together for good to those who love God, to those who are the called according to his purpose' (Romans 8:28). There are many things we cannot know; we have no idea what God may be calling us to; but to be able to say 'I know whom I have believed', is to be 'persuaded that he is able to keep what I have committed unto him against that Day' (2 Timothy 1:12).

We will also see, thirdly, that this is a story about God's *provision*. Every point along this line that takes us from the beginning to the end of Ruth's story, is about God providing. It is all about God providing food when there is no food, and shelter when there is no shelter, and hope when there is no hope, and blessing when there is no blessing. Out of his inexhaustible riches and fullness he makes abundant provision for the needs of men and women. The Book of Ruth will teach us that God supplies all our needs according to the riches of his Glory by Christ. There is a God who is the great provider, but his providing is matched to his wisdom, for he does not give us everything that we want, but everything we need. It was to such a God as this that Ruth came, and it is to that God, that we too may come.

The setting

Now it came to pass, in the days that the judges ruled, that there was a famine in the land. Ruth 1:1

In the last chapter we looked at these opening words of this great book of the Old Testament, words that set for us both the focus and the context of this book. You will recall that we noted one or two points about this book, which is sandwiched for us between the Book of Judges and the first Book of Samuel; two of the great historical narratives of the Old Testament.

The Book of Ruth is one of the shortest in the Bible, and on the surface, it seems just to be concerned with a very simple romantic tale that centred around this woman from Moab. Yet, in the Book of Ruth we have the Gospel summarised for us as we see this woman, who was brought up far away from the land of covenant blessing and promise, brought into the bond of the covenant and into a relationship with God.

We also noted that the Book of Ruth speaks to us of God's providences in the lives of his people. He allows some sad situations and difficult circumstances into their experience. Elimelech and Naomi, with their sons Mahlon and Chilion went from Bethlehem to Moab; and there Naomi saw very hard things as she stood some years later beside the graves of her husband and her two sons. We are reminded here of the ways in which God visits his people with hardships in order to bring them to himself.

We are reminded too of how the purposes of God are worked out through all these providences. God accomplishes his eternal design in and through the history of this world and the experiences of men and women in it. None of these situations are wasted. Every one of them works for God's glory and our good, as they worked together for the good of Ruth and the good of Naomi, and at length for the good of the whole world. Unknown to her in these days in Moab, Ruth was to find a place in the genealogy of Jesus Christ. It was from her that the Saviour was to be descended.

We also noted that the Book of Ruth is set 'in the days when the judges ruled'. The period of the judges, of course, covered a considerable length of time, and perhaps the story of Ruth was quite early in that period. More important is the detail we are given of the way in which this period was characterised: 'In those days there was no king in Israel: every man did that which was right in his own eyes.'

The result of this self-reliance and independence from God was calamitous. Time and again in the Book of Judges, God delivered his people into the hands of their enemies, to teach them that no man can set himself up in autonomy or independence against God and prosper. God delivered his people into the hands of their enemies to bring them low, to bring them to repentance, to bring them to himself. They cried to God and God raised the judges who delivered them out of the hands of their enemies. But no sooner were they delivered than they were back, back to this independent spirit and this self-willed spirit that is the hallmark of the period (see Judges 2:11–23).

The Book of Ruth tells us that it was in these days that God sent a famine. It is this famine that precipitates the whole of the story of Ruth, that sets the ball rolling. It is this famine that leads to Elimelech and Naomi going with their families to Moab. It is this famine that sets off the chain of events that is going to lead to the graves in Moab, the decision to return, Ruth's coming back to Bethlehem, her entry into the fields of Boaz, her gleaning there, her marriage and at last her child and her family, and the blessing of God upon her.

Most of us who live in the Western world are strangers to the whole experience of famine, and I trust that we always will be, but the Bible often speaks of famine. For instance, when Joseph was Governor of Egypt, his brothers went there looking for food because there was a famine. Similarly, in those days of the judges, there was also a famine. I am going to pause there, because I believe that there is always a famine when there is independence from God. It is a principle of biblical teaching and of biblical theology that the moment a man moves away from the path of God's truth and the path of God's will, he is on the road to famine. It is absolutely clear in the word of God that there is no bread for anyone who walks the path of disobedience from God. That is precisely the point that is underlined for us here. Everyone did what was right in their own eyes. *That was when the famine came*, and it was also *why* the famine came. It was that famine and their reaction to it that brought Elimelech and Naomi with their sons to the land of Moab.

The Famine: God's Judgement

It is important to remind ourselves that God told his people time and time again throughout the Old Testament, that famine was one way by which he would judge them for their sins. This famine represented just such a judgement from God upon this particular generation.

Please do not misunderstand me. I know that there are places in the world that are ravaged by famine and by lack of natural resources, by lack of food and water. Often, people point to these phenomena and say, 'How can you believe in God if this is true?' I believe in the God of the Bible, who says to me that he will meet the needs of everyone that lives (Psalm 145:15–16). The God of the Bible tells me that the world has sufficient resources to meet the needs of every man, woman and child. God has made us stewards of the bounty and the richness and the provision with which he has favoured us. One reason why there are many people in the world who have nothing is our lack of stewardship and biblical handling of the vast resources that God has given us. The fact of famine is not an argument against God, it is an argument against ourselves!

Returning to the Bible, and to God's programme for the education of his own people in the Old Testament, God made it abundantly clear that famine represented his judgement on the sins of the nation. Do you remember that he intimated as much to Adam? The moment Adam fell, and broke covenant with God at the very dawn of human history, God said, 'Cursed is the ground for your sake' (Genesis 3:17–19). The garden of Eden had been a place where work was both easy and fulfilling, a place whose resources yielded everything that Adam and Eve needed to survive on; but sin destroyed the very metabolism of the creation and the very richness of the ground. Now a curse lay upon it, to the extent that the whole creation even now groans because of man's sin (Romans 8:22). With the unfolding of God's revelation throughout the Old Testament, we come back to this principle time and time again. Sin leads to curse and to judgement. One avenue of God's judgement is the very world which he designed and created. God's people sin against Him. What does he do? He sends them a famine. He cuts off the rain, and the staff of bread (see Leviticus 26:26; Psalm 105:16), the very resources that they need in order to survive. All this is because of how far from him they have actually gone.

God made this explicit in Deuteronomy 28, where God sets before his people the blessings of obedience and the curses on their disobedience. 'If you do not listen,' he says, 'then this is what is going to happen. You'll carry your seed into the field, much seed, and you'll gather but little in. The locusts will consume it. You will plant vineyards and dress them but you will neither drink of the wine nor gather the grapes because the worms will eat them. You'll beget sons and daughters but you'll not enjoy them: they'll go into captivity. The trees and the fruit of your land will be consumed by the locust' (Deut 28:39–42). Why is he going to do that? 'All these curses shall come upon you because you did not obey the voice of the Lord God' (verse 45). There is this direct relationship between the disobedience and the famine. They were going to be industrious in the field but would take little back; sowing their seed for little return; working the ground but having nothing to eat; diligent and industrious, yet starving, because they had not listened to the voice of their God.

It is important to see the link between cause and effect here. When they do not obey, they have no food. Where they reject the claims of God's truth, there will be a famine in the land. The same phenomenon is highlighted in Jeremiah 34:17. God accuses his people of failing to listen, and to proclaim his word. So, God says, 'I proclaim liberty to you—to the sword, to pestilence and to famine!' Here is a highly ironic touch. God is saying 'You want freedom? I'll give you freedom—freedom to starve because you have disobeyed me!'

In 2 Samuel 21:1 we are told that there was a famine in the days of David for three years. Not until the third year did David enquire of the Lord. God sent a famine in the second year but still David did not return to the Lord. It was only in the third year that he went and enquired of the Lord, 'Why is this famine happening to us?' God said, 'Because Saul slew the Gibeonites'. This famine is directly traceable to the disobedience of God's covenant people. Therefore, in the Old Testament, God educated his people regarding the seriousness and solemnity of sin by sending a famine on the land.

However, the prophet Amos talks about another famine: 'In those days,' says Amos, 'I will send a famine in the land. Not a famine of bread or of water but of hearing the Word of God' (Amos 8:11). That is the worst possible kind of famine. God says that because of the sins of the people, he is going to keep back not the rains from the heaven, not the goodness of the soil, but his very Word. The people have disobeyed, so now they will starve. Here is this fundamental principle of Old Testament theology: that the sin of rebellion and disobedience of the people of God led to starvation, both physical and spiritual.

There is a sense in which it is the same still. The moment we move away from the path of obedience is the moment our souls begin to starve. Is this not what we read in Psalm 106:15, when God gave the people their request, but sent leanness into their souls? God says about his people that he had let them out of Egypt and he had guided them and redeemed them, but they rebelled against him. There is this incorrigible tendency of the human heart to rebel against God, and the result is barrenness and leanness.

If you are not born again, your soul is starved. Jesus says to you on the pages of the Gospel that supposing we gained the world and lost our soul through our sin, it would profit us nothing. That is why Jesus is compared to bread, to food, and it is why the offer of the Gospel is portrayed so often (such as in Isaiah 55:1) as an invitation to a banquet. There is a feast to which starving souls can come, and there is bread from Heaven, which starving souls can eat.

Even for those of us who profess to love the Lord, is it not the case that often we too experience famine, which can be traced to our sin and to our self-will? Listen to God's lament in Psalm 81:13–15: 'O that my people would listen to me; that Israel would walk in my ways ... He would have fed them also with the finest of wheat'. We must remember that these great words were spoken of God's people. The moment we walk any other road but the road of God's path and God's will, is the moment famine begins to afflict our souls. When a man cannot eat he becomes weak. He loses his strength and can do nothing. It is all too possible for a Christian man or woman to stray far away from God, and to have spiritual starvation instead of spiritual nourishment, famine instead of feasting.

More than anything else, the modern evangelical church needs men and women who are infused by God, who are on fire by God, who have one great burning zeal and determination to walk the path of obedience to God's will and truth. It needs men and women who know that when their souls are lean, something is wrong.

There were many places in the history of the Church, where vast congregations gathered to hear the Word of God. These places are empty now. A famine has come; and it has come because the church drifted so far from the path of God's truth that God plucked his candlestick away, just as he threatened to do in the case of Ephesus (Revelation 2:5). You know, the Epistle to the Ephesians does not contain even a hint that anything was wrong in that congregation; yet by the time John writes Revelation—within a generation—the Gospel has been watered down and the witness of the church compromised. God is threatening to remove the light of Gospel truth and Gospel preaching.

Can we not see the same thing evident in the history of the church of Christ in Scotland and in England and even throughout the nations of the world? Are there not many places that once burned with zeal and enthusiasm for the things of God but there is nothing there now. God once said, 'My spirit will not always strive with man' (Genesis 6:3). He sent the famine and removed the blessing. The famine of Ruth 1:1 spoke of God's judgement. It spoke of the people's sin, and of their distance from God.

The Famine: God's Call

The famine was not simply a register of the fact that something was wrong; it was a call from God to get things right! It was a trumpet sound—God's judgement was in the earth so that men would fear him and return to him by renewing their relationship with him.

What happened following the threatened curses of Deuteronomy 28? God renewed the covenant with his people in Deuteronomy 29! What was the essential thing? 'Therefore keep the words of this covenant and do them, that you may prosper in all that you do' (Deuteronomy 29:9). Sin brings adversity; obedience brings prosperity!

This is not the prosperity Gospel of some American televangelists, who preach riches and material possessions as the reward for faith in Christ. No; the prosperity God promises is a spiritual one. Just as the famine highlighted a spiritual need, so repentance and obedience would lead to spiritual renewal and revival.

Listen to what Jesus says in the Sermon on the Mount. The one thing that will permit a soul to enter Heaven is obedience to God's will. 'Many will come to me,' he says, 'in that day and say 'Lord, Lord, we prophesied, and we cast out devils and we performed miracles and we did many wonderful works' (Matthew 7:22). He will turn to them and say, 'Not everyone who says, 'Lord, Lord' will enter into my Kingdom, but he who does the will of my father who is in Heaven.' Do you see the emphasis? It is not on prophesying, or on preaching, or on casting out devils. It is not about performing miracles. Important as these things are, Jesus says that a man can do them all and be lost.

The apostle Paul reminded himself of that constantly. Congregation planter and evangelist though he was, he said that he fought 'not as one who beats the air, but I discipline my body and bring it into subjection, lest, when I have preached to others, I myself should become disqualified' (1 Corinthians 9:27). It is possible, says the New Testament, to have a life that has all the apparent evidences of saving grace and Christian piety, and yet be a stranger to grace and to God. Our usefullness in the kingdom is no guarantee of our belonging to it.

The call and claims of the Gospel are to men and women who know that obedience matters. They know that even when they themselves fail, the one place to which they must come, is to the God against whom they have sinned. David sinned grievously against God, yet in Psalm 51 he comes with his broken heart, with repentance, with grief and hatred of his sin, as the Westminster Shorter Catechism puts it, to the God he has offended. He knows that burnt offerings will not suffice (Psalm 51:16); religious observance is not enough. He knows that he needs to get right with God and begin all over again to love and serve the Lord, because to obey is better than to sacrifice (1 Samuel 15:22).

Thus part of the purpose of this famine was to renew obedience. It was the voice of God speaking loudly to the souls of his people, calling them to return and repent. Yet for the most part they failed to hear, and failed to obey. And, as we shall see, they paid a high price for continuing obstinately in the path of sin.

The mistake

A certain man of Bethlehem, Judah, went to sojourn in
the country of Moab, he and his wife and his two sons.
Ruth 1:1

We have spent some time looking at the two important markers at the beginning of this Book of Ruth which set the context for us.

First of all the writer tells us that the Book of Ruth was set in 'the days when the judges ruled'; and we took note of the fact that at the very end of the Book of Judges we have a summary of this period, 'in those days there was no king in Israel, every man did that which was right in his own eyes'. The one great characteristic of this period was the general rebellion against the authority of God, his law and his word. I have suggested that this is one of the reasons that the Book of Ruth is so relevant to us in our society. We too are living in a day when the authority of God's word has been despised and neglected, and men and women have a reduced view of the supremacy of the Scriptures. We are called to maintain the absolute standards of God's word. God does not allow us to do what is right in our own eyes. There are only two eyes that matter, and these are the eyes of God, that are able to look right into the depths of a man's soul. The Bible is calling us to remember that the eyes of God are in all the earth (2 Chronicles 16:9), and that the God who is not blind cannot be mocked (Galatians 6:7).

The second great characteristic was this famine: 'there was a famine in the land.' That was not some accident of providence, some unfortunate disaster that afflicted the nation. The Bible, you will recall, throughout the Old Testament, makes it very clear that famine in God's land is a chastisement for the sin of his people. It is his judgement upon them because they have sinned against Him. He does not tolerate their independent, self-willed, rebellious spirit forever, and sends a famine to the land, even into the place that flowed with milk and honey.

Indeed, part of the irony of the opening words of this chapter is here, in the statement that there was 'a man from Bethlehem' around whom the opening events will revolve; because Bethlehem means 'the house of bread'. It was a place where God blessed his people, and ultimately it was to this place that the bread of life was to come when Jesus was born into this world and became incarnate in our nature. Yet here is the house of bread lacking bread. God has denied his people their very sustenance. He has done it not because he is some kind of capricious God, some kind of self-willed deity who delights to see people suffering. This famine has one end in view; God is calling his people to repent and return to him.

It was this famine that really sparked off the whole chain of events that led to the conversion of Ruth and to her coming from the land of Moab to the house of bread. The first event in this chain was that Elimelech took his family away from Bethlehem to Moab when this famine was in the land. I think it is interesting that Elimelech is not named at this particular point in verse one; he is described as 'a certain man'. I think the significance of that is this: Elimelech was probably not the only man who made this journey from Bethlehem to Moab. He may well have been one of many who took their families away from Bethlehem to Moab because they knew there was plenty of food there, and amongst the many men that went to Moab there was a certain man of Bethlehem-Judah who went with his wife and his two sons.

Then at verse two, we are told that his name was Elimelech, the name of his wife was Naomi, his two sons Mahlon and Chilion, Ephrathites of Bethlehem. That means that they were of the stock of Abraham's race. They were, in the words of Paul, 'Hebrews of the Hebrews' (Philippians 3:5). There was no mixed blood in their family; they were genuine members of God's covenant people, Ephrathites of Bethlehem. They came into the country of Moab and the Bible says that 'there they continued'.

I do not want to labour these opening verses but it is, I think, vitally important that we grasp what is happening here, because we cannot appreciate the story of Ruth until we understand the story of Elimelech. Part of the significance of this man's story is in his name. The name Elimelech means 'my God is king'. There was a priest in the Old Testament who was called Eli: that is the Hebrew for 'my God'. The word 'melech' is the Hebrew for *king*. This man carries a great name. He is named after the God of the covenant; his name signifies that the God of the covenant is his sovereign Lord.

If this story tells us anything, it tells us that a name is not enough. John was called by God in the Book of Revelation to write seven letters to the churches throughout Asia, and to one of them, God said, 'You have a name that you are alive but you are dead' (Revelation 3:1). This church had a reputation and a denomination (a denomination simply means that she had a name). Most Christians have attachments to particular denominations or congregations. We may be Presbyterians, or Baptists, or Anglicans, or none of the above. Our names may carry their reputations with them. But God's message to the church in Sardis was that a name is not enough. It is not enough to have a good name and to be able to say 'I belong to this denomination'; not if we are spiritually dead or spiritually comatosed. It's not enough for a Christian to have a name, to have the profession and to wear a badge advertising that he is a Christian. The acid test goes much, much deeper.

The story of Elimelech tells us of the great distance there can be between a man's reputation and the reality of his private, personal relationship with God. This brings us to the very heart of the Bible's teaching. There was a man in the New Testament who had a great name, a great religion and great standing in his religion; he was a leader amongst his people. Nicodemus came to Jesus at night and said to him 'We know that you are a teacher come from God. No man can do those works that you do unless God is with him' (John 3:2). Jesus is not prepared to enter into this religious discussion with Nicodemus, who has come to the Lord with his own agenda. Jesus says to him 'Unless a man is born again, he will never see the Kingdom of God.' It does not matter what name Nicodemus has. The test is—has he been changed from the inside? Is his will captured to obedient service to Christ?

There is a sense in which every Christian bears the name of Elimelech. Paul says in 1 Corinthians 12:3: 'No man speaking by the spirit of God calls Jesus accursed. And no man can say that Jesus is Lord, except by the spirit.' Paul is telling us that if we have the spirit of God in our heart, Jesus Christ is our Lord and our God and our king. True Christianity, true biblical religion bows like Thomas did at the feet of Jesus and says 'My Lord and my God' (John 20:28). That is the badge of Christian profession.

Is it the reality? Is a name all we have? Does our profession have substance and meaning? Or does our life argue against our profession? Do our actions and our words and our behaviour in our homes and our families and our communities, argue against the very profession we are making as Christians?

What is it that belies Elimelech's reputation to be subject to the sovereignty of God? It is simply this: that he went to Moab. On the surface of it there were many reasons why he should go to Moab. He had a family to look after—a wife and two sons to care for— and there was no bread in Bethlehem. It was only logical that he, as a responsible husband and father, should take his family elsewhere. So they went to the country of Moab. If he had not gone to the country of Moab his sons would not have married. His son would not have married Ruth. Ruth the Moabitess would never have come to Bethlehem. Surely it was God's will that Elimelech should go to Moab?

There is a fundamental principle of behaviour brought before us again and again in the Bible, and it is this: *you cannot justify an action by its consequences*. God is able to bring good out of evil, to make even sin work for good in the experience of his people; but we cannot justify an action by the blessings that may follow it. Perhaps Naomi could have said to herself, 'At the end of the day, well, it was good for us to go to Moab. There we met Ruth who came with us.' I know that, and I know that this family enjoyed blessings that God gave them out of his grace and out of his kindness, but I am still going to insist that nothing can justify the decision that Elimelech took to go to Moab at all. It was fundamentally wrong.

Let me apply this in one or two practical ways. I have heard people try to justify having women in the ministry because they received a blessing from hearing a woman preach. That may or may not be right; I am not going to deny that they received a blessing, but if they did, it was *in spite of* the action and not because of it. You cannot justify the action from the consequences: the Bible makes it very clear that the ministry of the Gospel is for males only in the church of Jesus Christ. The issue is not whether or not people have had blessing from women preachers; the issue is—what does God say? Does he not say through Paul 'I suffer not a woman to teach?' That ought to be the end of the matter.

I have heard people justify Christians marrying non-Christians because blessing came from it. Maybe the unconverted husband was converted and found the Lord; maybe their children grew up to know the Lord. God is able to use all of these things to fulfil his purposes; but the Bible is clear that there are 'unequal yokes' into which believers are not to enter (2 Corinthians 6:14). So, whatever course of action you follow, whether it is in your own personal life, or in the life of your church, it must have the sanction of the Word of God. I know that there are difficult questions relating to the subject of guidance; and I know that there are issues over which the Bible seems to be silent. However, there are other issues where the Bible is not silent, and we dare not go against the mind of God speaking to us in Scripture, not even on the grounds that others did it and were blessed. I am going to argue here that it is impossible to justify the action of Elimelech in going to Moab; even though blessings followed, and even though Ruth was converted, the decision to leave was wrong.

Perhaps I should say at this point that one thing the story does tell us is that God rules over all. In a strange way, Elimelech's name could stand as the theme of the whole book! God IS king! Even when we disobey his command, and walk contrary to his will, he over-rules every experience for his own glory and the good of his people. He has revealed his will in the Bible, and if we are truly born again we will wish to acknowledge God's sovereignty in loving obedience and service for him. Yet he has purposes which he has not revealed to us; and perhaps what shows us God's kingship more than anything is the fact that even our disobedience is over-ruled by him.

Is that not a great comfort to you—I know it is to me! There are areas in my life when I go far astray, and come far short of what God wants me to be. Yet in his grace, he over-rules my sin, and permits me to fall and allows me to disobey, so that he will show that he truly is in charge. Elimelech's name at one and the same time both condemns his personal action, which was a transgression against the God of the covenant, and sets for us the great lesson of this book. I believe that in the Book of Ruth we see that God is actually king. He does rule. I believe that Ruth came to know the Lord as a result of God's overruling grace, although her story begins with her father-in-law whose name said that he was subject to the kingship of God and yet he lived as though he were not. This man whose name said 'the God of the covenant is my sovereign', acted in a way that went directly to the contrary of the command of that very sovereign.

Elimelech heard the voice of the king

Elimelech was a man who heard the voice of God speaking to his soul. He was part of God's covenant people, God's covenant community there in the house of bread in Bethlehem, and he heard the voice of God.

He heard it, I think, in at least two ways. He heard the voice of God first in the famine. He heard the voice of God in this crisis of providence that God sent among his people when he cut off the supply of bread, and they had absolutely nothing. That, as we saw, was God's voice to his people. It was God's convicting voice, God's chastising voice, God's voice in judgement, God calling them back to himself, back to repentance, back to the God from whom they had strayed. The famine was the herald of God, awakening his people to see their sin and their rebellion and their waywardness.

Elimelech heard that voice—perhaps you have too. Perhaps there were times of crisis in your life—things that you never dreamt would happen, things that you never wanted, things that came into your life so completely unexpectedly and they had the effect of turning your whole life and home and thinking right upside down. Perhaps illness struck and stayed; death came in and took away loved ones and your home was never the same again.

How many times has the voice of God come your way? When disaster struck, and you had your share of disappointments, when some things that you had planned and hoped for fell crashing to the ground—this was not the way you wanted it and not the way you planned—God was saying to you that it was time for you to bow before him. It was time for you to say with Abraham 'shall not the judge of all earth do right' (Genesis 18:25). To say with Job 'the Lord gave and the Lord has taken away, blessed be the name of the Lord' (Job 1:21). To say with the Apostle Paul, 'I know that the sufferings of this present time are not worthy to be compared with the glory that shall be revealed' (Romans 8:18). How often does God bring home to us the most majestic truths about himself, as well as the glaring truth about ourselves, not in the School of Peace and Pleasure, but in the University of Grief and Pain?

Elimelech heard these truths in the providence that determined a famine on the land. God was calling his people to account and to attention, to repentance and renewal. Yet they did not hear.

There was more. Elimelech heard the voice of God not just in his providence; he heard the voice of God in the Bible too. We have already noted that these were not people without a Bible; God had given them his law long before this. The law had been preserved for them: written by Moses, preserved by Joshua and recounted time and time again in their hearing, and part of that law had a direct bearing on the situation of God's people at this point. You see, God forbade his people to have anything to do with Moab!

Do you recall what the Moabites had done when the children of Israel were wandering in the wilderness? They refused to give them bread and water (Deuteronomy 23:4; Nehemiah 13:2). Balak, the king of Moab, called for Balaam to come and to curse Israel but he couldn't (Numbers 23:7ff). Israel enjoyed the blessing of God, and to curse them was futile. As far as Moab was concerned, God said in Deuteronomy 23:3, 'do not have anything to do with the Moabites or the Ammonites in all your generations, forever.' This was on the very eve of the Israelite occupation of Caanan; and at this crucial turning-point in their history God said to them, 'these are people from whom you are to be separated. These are people with whom you are not permitted to mix. These are a people to whom you are not to give your sons to marry their daughters or your daughters to marry their sons.' The law was written plainly and clearly: 'An Ammonite or Moabite shall not enter the congregation of the Lord for ever' (Deuteronomy 23:3).

God is jealous of the distinctiveness of his own church; and his call to his people is this: 'come out from among them and be separate' (2 Corinthians 6:17, referring to Numbers 33:51–56). In God's army you cannot nail your colours to a fence; you cannot sit in no-man's land, with one foot in the world and one foot in the Kingdom of Grace. God calls his people out of darkness and in to the kingdom of light, so that they will stand unreservedly and boldly on the side of Jesus in this world, not compromised in their religion but standing firmly in defence of God and his word, his cause, his name and his day.

So Elimelech had it there in the Bible. God prohibited relationships between his people and the Moabites. Is it not interesting that when the people of God, under the governorship of Nehemiah, returned from the exile in Babylon, Nehemiah took them back to that very passage in Deuteronomy 23 when he saw that in his absence the Jews had allowed their families to marry and intermingle with the Moabites and the Ammonites. (Nehemiah 13). It is just not meant to be. God's people are called to be distinctive and to be distinctively holy. That is the call of the Gospel, and Elimelech heard it. He heard it in his providence, he heard it in the precepts of the Bible; and you've heard it too. Has God not called you to take up the cross and to follow Jesus? To 'leave your father's house because the king desires you' (Psalm 45:10–11). Do you know what it is to be so caught up in your heart with the burning attractiveness of Jesus Christ? To know him and love him with such an intensity of devotion that you will follow Jesus Christ, come what may?

Elimelech silenced the voice of the king

The tragedy of Elimelech's story is that he silenced the voice of God. The famine called him to repent, but he did not repent. The famine called the people back to God, but many of them, Elimelech included, did not turn back to God. The famine said to them, 'it's time for you to get your relationship with God right'. They did not get their relationship with God right; instead they went to Moab and they flew full in the face of the direct precepts and prohibitions of God's word.

Why did they do that? Why did Elimelech do that? Why did he go to Moab when God's word said 'Don't go to Moab'? Why did he turn away from Bethlehem, when God sent the famine to call his people back to himself? There was one fundamental reason for it. Moab had bread, and Bethlehem did not. Elimelech is reasoning it out in his mind and saying, 'We need bread'. So he takes his wife and family to Moab looking for bread, because there is bread there.

Elimelech is addressing the wrong problem. The problem was not the lack of bread! The problem was the lack of a right relationship with God.

This was not the first famine in the history of God's people. Listen to the summary of Psalm 105:16–19.

Moreover He called for a famine in the land; he destroyed all the provision of bread. He sent a man before them—Joseph—who was sold as a slave. They hurt his feet with fetters, he was laid in irons, until the time that his word came to pass; the word of God tested him…

The same God who had sent the famine, sent the provision. He was not about to leave his people in abject despair. No, he provided for them. He raised up a Joseph, whom they despised and neglected and cast into prison. Yet Joseph was the one through whom God gave them bread. The history of God's church is a history of supernatural, gracious provision on the part of God. If he sends a famine, it's not forever; he will provide bread for his people.

Elimelech is not going to wait for God's bread. He is going to go for Moab's bread. He is just walking by sight, not by faith. He is living for the here and now, for what his eye can see and for what his heart wants, for what his appetite craves. In spite of the clear message of the famine, and the clear counsel of the Bible, Elimelech yields to the temptation to disobey God and to distrust his provision.

James tells us that that is exactly how sin works in human life. A man is tempted this way: he first lusts after something. He sees it and desires it and 'lust, when it conceives,' says James, 'brings forth sin' (James 1:15). Sin is the child of lust. Sin is never the child of faith. So here is Elimelech, with his name, 'my God is king'. Yet in spite of his professed allegiance to the God of the covenant, he desires bread and goes about getting it in a way that is directly contrary to the prescriptive will of God.

The Bible, however, calls us to live the life of faith. That means looking and trusting to things we cannot see with the natural eye. The Bible is calling us to trust in Jesus Christ. We cannot see him with our natural eye, but the Bible says he is alive; that he came into this world and died and was buried and is now at the right hand of God. The Bible asks us to live by faith in that Christ. It says to us 'Believe in the Lord Jesus Christ' (Acts 16:31).

Elimelech's desire for food leads to his disobedience and his moving further and further away from God, but the road to Moab does not solve the problem. Elimelech only complicates the problem, and brings the problem with him. You see, *the heart of Elimelech's problem is the problem of Elimelech's heart*. We may change our circumstances, as Elimelech did, and try to go off in a different direction, just like Elimelech did, but until we deal with the problem of our heart's relationship with God, we will never deal with our problem. So Elimelech leaves Bethlehem looking for a solution, but he is only getting deeper and deeper into his problem.

There is only one place where burdens are lifted and problems dealt with, and that is at the cross of Jesus Christ. Isn't that how John Bunyan painted his pilgrim, Christian, in *Pilgrim's Progress*? When Christian came at last to the cross, the burden that he had been carrying from the city of destruction all along the way rolled right off him, away down into the grave, into the tomb. There, near the cross, he says,

Must here be the beginning of my bliss?
Must here the burden roll from off my back?
Must here the strings that bound it to me crack?
Blessed cross. Blessed sepulchre. Blessed rather be
the man that was put to shame for me.'

Do you know anything of that? There is peace in Christ, a fullness of grace in him that means that whatever our burdens and trials, he will give us grace to face each day and cross each difficult valley. Burdens are lifted at Calvary. They are dealt with when you bring them to Jesus, but they are never dealt with when you take them to Moab. Going to Moab only compounds the problem. It may offer a quick solution, but in the end will bring only more heartache and sorrow.

Martin Luther experienced this very thing when he was a priest in the Roman Catholic church. There he was, working out his salvation, climbing stone steps on his knees to get rid of his burden. But the burden was still there. He had not got to the root of the problem, which was the problem of his heart, and he did not get to the root until he came to the cross. Romans 5 told him that if we are justified by faith, we have peace with God; the burden is lifted and it rolls away. There is peace for those who are justified, and only for those who are justified. There is no peace, God says, for the wicked (Isaiah 48:22; 57:21).

Elimelech lost the voice of God

Eventually they came into the country of Moab and, we are told, 'remained there … and Elimelech died'. 'Lust,' says James, 'when it conceives, brings forth sin, and sin when it is finished, brings forth death.' There is always death as a result of sin. Sin never yielded a positive return. Life and peace never came out of sin. Out of sin there comes a grave, there comes a broken heart, there come tears and mourning and regret, there comes bitterness instead of blessing. Naomi went with Elimelech to Moab and ended up weeping at the grave of her late husband, because death always follows sin.

That is why the Saviour died, to deal with sin, and to deal with it on its own territory. As Hebrews 2:14 puts it, Jesus took flesh and blood so that through death he might destroy the devil. He took the nature of those who were subject to death, in order that he might go into death's territory and conquer sin and death for ever. He went right into the grave to destroy the power of sin, and he comes out from the grave, having dealt with sin, having risen with victory and with power. Sin is robbed of its sting, the grave of its victory, because the Lord has died.

Are we living as Paul desired to live, knowing the power of Christ's resurrection (Philippians 3:10)? Have we learned the victory that comes through faith in Christ? Or are we still prone to live the flesh life—tempted by our own lusts and sinful desires to move away from God as Elimelech did? Let's seek for God's help and grace to rise above sin's power and to live in heavenly realms, experiencing peace and blessing in our souls.

The test

Then they lifted up their voices and wept again; and Orpah kissed her mother-in-law but Ruth clung to her. Ruth 1:14

We have watched Elimelech, the husband of Naomi, bring his wife and family out of the land of Bethlehem to dwell in the country of Moab. I suggested that it was a very grievous sin on Elimelech's part for him to do what he did. God had forbidden his people to have any contact with the Moabites or with the Ammonites, and he had also told them that a famine was one of the means by which he would visit the sins of his people, but instead of turning back to God, and acknowledging their sin, Elimelech brought Naomi and their sons Mahlon and Chilion to the land of Moab.

Naomi, however, was not long in the land of Moab when she discovered the hard lesson for herself that sin can only produce death. The eyes of the family had been fixed on the apparent richness of Moab, but there Elimelech died and Naomi was left with her two sons. They married wives from Moab, named Orpah and Ruth. The story then jumps forward to a point ten years later, when Mahlon and Chilion died, and Naomi, Orpah and Ruth were left together as widows in Moab. The family had left Bethlehem-Judah and they had come to Moab expecting to find great things; instead all that they found were broken hearts and broken dreams, and sore experiences under God's hand.

The Book of Ruth teaches us that God can bring good out of evil, and blessing out of sin. It does not teach us to continue in sin so that grace might abound (cf. Romans 6:1), but it does shows us that where sin increased, grace increased all the more (Romans 5:20). Elimelech had to leave Bethlehem so that Ruth would go there. Mahlon and Chilion had to leave Bethelehem so that Obed, the father of Jesse, the father of David, would be reared in these hallowed precincts, in the land of Judah. One generation makes way for another because God's purpose is like a stream through the desert-places of history; and although Satan might have momentary victories with us, God in Christ will win the war. Satan wants nothing more than that we should turn our back on God and his covenant, but it is never a good path to follow. Sin always brings loss. However, God's grace will triumph, even where sin abounds.

The lesson of the Book of Ruth is that there is a river running throughout all the events of history, winding its way both to the mountain tops of blessing and into the valleys of despair and desolation. That river of God's covenantal purposes is going to work out for the good of Ruth, and ultimately for the good and the salvation of the whole Church. It was from Ruth that David was born and it was from the line of David that Christ came. So one of the most important lessons we learn from this part of God's word is that even the darkest events of our lives have their role to play in the unfolding and the revealing of God's gracious purposes of salvation.

Before we go on, however, I want to draw your attention to the use of words in this book. We have already noted that Elimelech's name is significant. There are other words that are significant too. When the Holy Spirit of God inspired the scriptures, he gave the words. The Bible was not an arbitrary collection of religious ideas, but the word of God given in the words of men. The Spirit of God superintended the writing of these words, so that as the holy writers of the Old Testament penned the sacred Scriptures, the thoughts of God were given expression in the words of men. The writers were borne by the Spirit of God (2 Peter 1:21). So it was not just the general idea that was inspired, but the very words themselves.

When we study the language of this book, there is a very interesting word usage. When the Book of Ruth refers to Judah, the word that is used to describe Judah is the word 'land'; 'there was a famine in the *land*,' we read in verse one. In verse seven we read that they returned to their own *land*, to the land of Judah, but whenever Moab is mentioned in this chapter, the word that is used is the word *country*. 'There was a famine in the *land* of Judah so Elimenech went to sojourn in the *country* of Moab' (verse 1); 'they came into the *country* of Moab and remained there' (verse 2); 'Naomi heard in the *country* of Moab how the Lord visited his people,' (verse 6), so she went back 'to the *land* of Judah' (verse 7).

That is a very interesting distinction. The word that is translated in this chapter as 'land' is used almost three hundred times in the Bible to describe the whole earth, or the whole world. It is a word that describes a vast expanse of territory, whereas the word 'country' is a word that means a defined, limited, and allotted portion of territory.

So the Hebrew describes these events very carefully. There was a famine in the [vast] land of Judah and they went to the [limited] territory of Moab. It is almost as if the writer is telling us that God's wayward people left Bethlehem with the thought that Moab was going to give them so much. They thought that Moab was so full, and that it held a promise of great riches and vast blessings. They did not realise that the moment they departed from Judah they left the greater for the lesser, the unlimited for the limited. The land of covenant blessing, however small a physical geographical area it may have been, represented a vast world of God's great blessings of salvation. They left the great inheritance that God gave to his people, to go to a limited portion of Moab that promised so much, but could give them so little.

I suppose that the day, ten years after her husband died, when Naomi stood there with her two daughters-in-law, these young widows from Moab, she realised just how small Moab really was. They had left Judah a whole decade before this, with a great prospect in view, but Moab could give them nothing but a little tiny corner in which to bury their beloved dead. Moab gave them grief and tears, heartache, sorrow and loss. Those who have their inheritance in the glory know that that is always what Moab does.

People think that to become a Christian is to become narrow-minded, whereas what the Bible says is that it is the Christian who knows the blessing of fullness and vastness and liberty and release and freedom. It is the man who is still in his sins who is confined; he remains chained and limited in what he can do and in what he can achieve and in where he can go. Let's never forget that. It's the man who lives in his sins that is narrow-minded, not the Christian! The man who forsakes God is the man who has forsaken the vastness of God's covenant blessings for all the empty promises of Moab. In Psalm 73, Asaph confesses that he envied the wicked, who appeared to be prospering in the world, whereas, after all his years of devoted service and worship, Asaph himself had nothing but grief, heartache and tears. Yet when he saw things from God's perspective he realised that the wicked were the impoverished ones; and, indeed, he saw that the little they had would eventually be taken from them. Asaph was the truly rich man.

How we need to keep that perspective of faith! Otherwise we will be under the tyranny of our circumstances. For God's people in the Old Testament, the land was an integral part of God's covenant provision. Abraham had gone out from Ur in obedience to God, who promised him a place where he would dwell (Genesis 12:1; 15:7). As Hebrews 11:8–10 makes clear, Abraham's inheritance was not simply a portion of land in this world, but a spiritual inheritance—a city with foundations, built by God (Hebrews 11:10). Thus when God's people in the Old Testament came into possession of the land of Canaan, it symbolised all the spiritual blessings that now belong to the people of God, whose ultimate destination in glory with Christ is represented in the New Testament as a New Jerusalem (Revelation 3:12; 21:2). We have inherited Canaan! Let us not trade its blessings for the poor fare of Moab.

It was in the country of Moab that Naomi heard the news that was to change her attitude and the whole course of her life. She heard how the Lord had visited the land of Judah; he had visited his people and given them bread. God's famines in the experience of his people, are never permanent. They are seasonal. The chastening is not forever, but for the moment.

There is something else here. Naomi did not hear this news on a television bulletin or by e-mail. There was no instant communication. It took a while for the news to filter through from the land of Judah to the country of Moab that the famine was ended and that the house of bread had bread once again. So all the time that God's people were feasting on bread in Judah, Naomi was starving in Moab. The events remind us of the prodigal son of Luke 15 who had left his father's house, wasted his money and ended up sharing food with pigs. Yet all that time his father's servants were feasting on the bread that was there, which was overflowing in its abundance.

God's blessings are there for us to enjoy, and if we do not make use of them, we will be the poorer. Why should we go hungry when there is bread enough and to spare in our father's house? Why should we court sin, and Satan, and self, when in Jesus Christ there is a fullness of grace which will be enough for us? The moment we turn away from God we become lean, and hungry. Yet all the while those who remain faithful to him are making use of his constant supply of grace. Why should we go without when the storehouse of his grace and goodness overflows?

God was good to Naomi. He gave her the opportunity to return. He does not promise to give us such an opportunity. He says that this is our moment, our time for repentance. Naomi heard that God visited his people, then she arose. What a blessing she arose and went when she did! What a blessing that she took charge of her life and left Moab, and went back to the land of Judah. What about you? Is it time for you also to wake up to the reality of your situation and your need?

When Naomi left the country of Moab for the land of Judah, her daughters-in-law went with her. So in this first chapter, three testimonies converge: the story of Orpah, the story of Naomi, and the story of Ruth.

Have you noticed that these three women all wept on the way? Naomi talked with Orpah and Ruth, and they with Naomi; then they lifted up their voice and *wept*. Orpah kissed her mother in law, but Ruth clung to her. Ruth and Orpah and Naomi left Moab behind, and went weeping on the road.

I think these three women shed very different kinds of tears. There is a sense in which they were all tears of regret. Orpah regretted that she had ever left Moab at all; the pull of Moab was so strong on her heart and her life that she soon went back to her people and back to her gods. Naomi regretted that she had ever left Bethlehem, the land of covenant promise; hers were tears of repentance, tears that were bringing her back to the God from whom she had strayed, back to the land that she had left behind. But the tears of Ruth were tears of regret too; regret that she had never left Moab long before this. All she wanted now was to go with Naomi to enjoy the blessings of God's provision in Bethlehem, the house of bread. So the journey from Moab soon became a parting of the ways.

Orpah's story

Orpah accompanied Naomi and Ruth as they left Moab, but she found it surprisingly easy to return, to go back to the land of Moab where she had grown up and which she knew so well, whose people and whose gods held so much attraction for her. She lifted up her voice and she wept; but she still went back. She cried loudly, with strong tears on the way; but she still returned.

There is a sense, I suppose, in which she had really never left Moab at all. Her story tells us that beginning is not everything. Here was a woman who began, who set out. To all intents and purposes she turned her back on a former way of life, with all its attractions and all its idols. Had we seen her in the beginning of the journey, we might have thought that a change had come over Orpah. Had we seen her tears flowing, her voice lifted up as Naomi spoke to her on the roadside, her walk as she left Moab and took the road down towards Bethlehem, we would have said, 'Orpah? Orpah's a changed person.'

The tragedy was that Orpah was not a changed person. It is very possible for us to shed Orpah tears, and to do exactly what Orpah did. We can have great emotional and moving experiences, all of which give the promise of better things and of genuine change. Orpah heard, because Naomi heard, that God had visited the land of Judah and given his people bread. She knew that God's voice was speaking to her soul, and she left Moab. But it is all too possible to set out from Moab and yet go back to Moab.

Every ending has a beginning. For Ruth to come to the land of Bethlehem meant that she had to leave Moab. For every sinner to enter into the portals of glory at the end of life, means having to begin to take up the cross and to follow Jesus in this world. However, not every beginning, if it's a false beginning, has that kind of ending. It is impossible, we read in Hebrews 6:4, for those who were enlightened once upon a time to have their repentance renewed if they fall away. Such people have had experience of the power of the Gospel in their hearts and in their souls, they have 'tasted the powers of the world to come,' and experienced the heavenly gift. These experiences were the direct result of the influence of the Gospel on their lives, in their homes and on their souls. They had privileges that others did not have. They saw things that others did not see and they heard things that others didn't hear, and they felt things that others did not feel. Because God stepped in, at one point, to show them the meaning and glory of the Gospel, they cried with tears of remorse for the past and hope for the future. However, their hope, like their tears, was a false one. They were like the seed in the parable which fell by the wayside, and among the stones, and the thorns, and for a little while, it gave great promise because it sprang up (Luke 8:5–7). To all intents and purposes, the Gospel was going to succeed in the lives of these men and women. Until, that is, the sun beat down, and the testing time came, until it proved too difficult; then it was clear that there was no root, nothing under the surface at all, and it withered away. It is possible, says the New Testament, to start out like Orpah, to sweep out the devil that has been resident in your soul, to use the Lord's illustration in Luke 11:26. It is possible to sweep a devil out of your life, to reform your habits and to change your practices only to see seven devils worse than the first coming in again.

What matters is not so much how we begin; sometimes I confess I get a little concerned about hearing testimonies, because they focus so much on beginnings. As I have said, without beginnings we can have no endings, but what matters is that having begun, we might continue following the Saviour. Along the road from Moab to Judah, there are many Orpahs shedding tears of promise, with emotional and traumatic experiences that seem to signify the beginnings of a new interest. Deep down her heart was still with her own people and with her own gods.

It is an interesting detail in the parable of the pharisee and the publican in Luke 18:9–14 that Jesus did not commend the publican for coming to the temple. It was good that he was in the temple: he wanted to meet with God, and the temple was the right place for him. But Jesus commended him for the way he went home! 'I tell you, this man went home justified' is what Jesus said in Luke 18:14. And if there is one thing that is more important than our coming to church, it is the way we go home afterwards. Because to go home without any interest in Christ, is to run the risk, in the words of Hebrews 6:6, of 'crucifying the Son of God afresh.'

Naomi's story

So Orpah set out and soon returned; her tears were tears of regret that she had ever left Moab at all. Naomi shed tears too; she lifted up her voice and wept with her daughters-in-law as she reasoned with them about what had happened to her: 'the hand of God,' she says, 'has gone out against me.' She knew that it was for her sin and the sin of Elimelech that all this evil had come upon them. 'It grieves me much for your sakes, that the hand of the Lord has gone out against me' (1:13).

It is a very interesting thing, that even knowing that God's blessing was on the land of Judah and his curse on the country of Moab, Naomi pleaded with her daughters-in-law to return. I wonder why she did that? I think there are two things we have to say about that.

The first thing is that what she did was wrong. God's blessing was not on Moab, God's blessing was on Judah. God's bread was not in Moab, it was in Bethlehem. Naomi, I suggest, was wrong to say to her daughters-in-law 'you go back.' I wonder if perhaps she was trying in some way to wipe out and to block out the memory of her own past? After all, these daughters-in-law were living symbols of her backsliding and the backsliding of Elimelech. God had said about the Moabites, 'Don't give your daughters to their sons, or your sons to their daughters.' By proscribing intermarriage in this way, the purity and holiness of the covenant community would be guarded. Yet here was Naomi going back to the land of Judah with two daughters-in-law from Moab. Their presence would be with her as an abiding symbol of her disobedience.

I think there may be many Christians like that in Christ's church. I am not saying that they are encouraging others to go back. What I mean is that they have spent so long chasing after sin and running away from God that even now, having found peace with God, the scars of these former days are with them still. They are not now what they once were; they have been washed, cleansed, justified and sanctified; yet their very lives and faces are etched with the symbols of their own disobedience and their own sin. Indeed, their greatest grief is that they gave sin and self and Satan the best years of their lives.

That is why it is so important to live by faith. Because, even though our lives may bear the scars of former battles, Christ has indeed dealt with our unforgiving past and our accusing conscience. What Christ does is to wipe that all away. Christ has cleansed from all unrighteousness, and has poured his oil into every scar of sin. We are justified and complete in him.

But I suspect that Naomi was afraid of carrying back to Judah with her the evidences of how far she had strayed from God. It is possible, after all, for good people to do foolish things. You would never have thought David would sleep with Bathsheba and murder her husband to cover up his sin (2 Samuel 11), but he did. Remember the disciples who argued in the Upper Room about who would be the greatest (Luke 22:24), or Peter, who denied the Lord (Luke 22:54–62). The best of believers sometimes do the most unexpected of things. You would never have thought that Naomi would have encouraged her daughters-in-law to go back to Moab, but she did.

But—and here is where we see the wonderful grace of God in action –there is something else we've got to say about this too. *What was a sin to Naomi became a test to Ruth and Orpah.* That's the way God works. The folly of her language became the test of Orpah's and Ruth's commitment. 'Go back,' she said to them. Even as she tried to cover the marks of her sin, God used this to distinguish between the principle of sin in the life of Orpah and the principle of grace in the life of Ruth. We do not read here that Naomi confessed her sin, or made her peace with God. I believe that that came later. What was a sin to her at this point was a test to her daughters-in-law. It is amazing how God tests the work of his grace in the hearts of his people. He may use even the sins of his people to act as such a test. Orpah fails the test and she goes back, but Ruth cannot go back. Her heart has been weaned away from Moab and even when Naomi tells her to return, she says, 'I can't return'. Even when Naomi says, 'Look at your sister-in-law, follow her,' Ruth says, 'I can't go back. There's nothing for me in Moab any more.'

I would love more than anything to hear men and women, boys and girls say, 'There's nothing for me in Moab any more.' Every Gospel preacher wants that response of people saying, 'No, I am going to cleave to the Gospel. Orpah may leave, but I am going to cleave to the Lord and go with Naomi to the glory of Bethlehem country and the land of blessing.'

So when the test comes; and Christ says as he said in John 6:67 'Will you also go away?', will we say with Peter, 'To whom shall we go? Christ has the words of eternal life.' Do we know anything of the voice of God speaking to our soul? And how have we responded to it? Have we resisted the voice of the Holy Spirit, drawn more to the empty vanities of a Moab life than to the blessings of a covenant life? The richness and the fullness are in Bethlehem. That is where Naomi is headed, and that is where Orpah loses out. We will look at Ruth's story in our next study.

The choice

Ruth said, 'Entreat me not to leave you, Or to turn back from following after you; For wherever you go, I will go; And wherever you lodge, I will lodge; Your people shall be my people, And your God, my God. Where you die, I will die, and there will I be buried. The Lord do so to me, and more also, If anything but death parts you and me.' When she saw that she was determined to go with her, she stopped speaking to her. Ruth 1:16–18

In our last study we left three ladies somewhere on the road between Moab and Bethlehem. Naomi heard in the land of Moab how God had given his people bread. The famine was over. There was now food enough once again in the land of Judah, so Naomi left Moab with her daughters-in-law, each of them having buried a little bit of their heart in the dust of Moab. Now the three widows had set out on another journey, leaving these scenes of heartache behind. Orpah wept, then retraced her steps to Moab and its ways. Naomi wept tears of repentance and faith. What of Ruth?

Ruth's story

There were tears in the eyes of Ruth. Something is going on deep in her soul that not even Naomi can see. The work of God's grace in the soul is so absolutely personal and so absolutely mysterious that it is lost to human eyes. Here Naomi is persuading these two daughters-in-law to go back to the land of Moab. I suggested that she was wrong to do that, but I suggested too, that God turned this into a test for these two women. Orpah showed her true colours and went back. But the work that was going on in the soul of Ruth was such a work that it could not be extinguished. Ruth had been so touched by the Word of God and by the witness of God in the life and testimony of Naomi, that when her mother-in-law said 'Go back,' Ruth replied, 'I can't go back.' When Naomi said, 'Follow your sister-in-law and go back to your mother's house,' Ruth said, 'I can't do that'.

So it was with tears in her eyes that Ruth made her great pledge to Naomi: 'Don't ask me to go back. Don't ask me to return.' There is a fundamental objection in the soul of Ruth to being asked to return. I think there are times when this is the sign that God is working in a human life. Not the tears, but the objection. It is not the weeping, not the display of emotionalism, but this deep-seated, fundamental objection that really shows what has happened in Ruth's life: when Naomi says 'Go back,' she says 'Don't ask me to do that. Don't ask me to go back.'

There is an interesting reflection of this situation in the law governing Hebrew servants in Exodus 21:1–11. In that passage, the law of Moses allowed for the release of a servant in the seventh year of his servitude. After six years of work, he was offered his freedom. Not every slave, however, wanted to take up the offer. The law allowed for the possibility that a servant may have grown to love his master. In this case, it was necessary for the slave to have a mark placed in his ear as a sign that he was in the service of his master for life (Exodus 21:6). This seems to be the background to the words of Psalm 40:6, which in turn is applied to Jesus Christ in Hebrews 10:5, where the reference to the mark in the ear is replaced with the words 'a body you have prepared for me'. In fulfilling the prophecy of the willing servant, Jesus took our human nature as both a sign of his determination to serve God, and as the means through which that service would be carried out.

In following the example of Jesus, we too are called to be God's servants. We are called to his service, and are made willing to do his bidding through his own work in our lives (Psalm 110:3; Philippians 2:13). When he offers us our freedom, will we not say with the Hebrew servant, 'I love my master … I will not go out …' (Exodus 21:5)? Will we not echo the words of Ruth, whose heart had been won over to the service of Jehovah—'don't urge me to leave you'.

We can see the same principle at work in the experience of Simon Peter when he follows the Lord Jesus. There are crowds following him. Many, many 'disciples' are absorbed in the teaching of Jesus of Nazareth, and all of a sudden the cutting edge of truth becomes too offensive and too difficult to bear. From that time, many of them 'walk no more with him'. Yet these were people who had made some kind of pledge and some kind of commitment to following Jesus Christ. But when the teaching became too offensive, and too unpalatable, when they could not endure sound doctrine, these people went back. It is at that point that Jesus turns to his disciples and says, 'Will you also go away?'

It is then that we read of this fundamental objection to the possibility of returning; it wells up in the heart of Peter and it expresses itself in these great words: 'Lord, to whom shall we go? You have the words of eternal life' (John 6:68). I think there are many people who, when they begin following Jesus Christ do not even know what is happening to them, and cannot put their finger on what is happening to them. They know that the Gospel is beginning to turn their world upside-down. They know that they are becoming absorbed in the Bible and in the Christ of the Bible more than ever they were, and yet they would not dare say that they had become Christians, but they know this: that were Jesus to offer them the freedom and the possibility of a return to Moab, they would object and say, 'No. I do not know what is going on in my soul and I'm not sure what my affections and my emotions are telling me, but this one thing I do know: there's nothing for me in Moab any more.'

Can you say that? This is the one, great, absolute test. Can you go back? Can you think of living without Jesus? You've been aware of him bringing you through many difficult experiences, many dark valleys, through very testing and very trying times, and you cannot go back. You would rather have him in the night than be without him in the sunshine. You'd rather have him in the storms than be without him when the winds are blowing gently. You would rather have him and know that he's yours and you are his and that bond is there, cemented in a covenant union forever, than live one moment without the Lord who has come into your soul by the power of his own grace. So will you say with Ruth, 'Whatever you ask me to do, don't ask me to live without Jesus. Don't ask me to even think of giving him up and going back to the gods of Moab, or to its people and pastimes.' Because, Ruth says, 'I know what I want. I know where my heart is and I know that what I want is in front of me and not behind me. I want to leave what's behind me there, and I want to press on towards the mark of the prize of the high calling of God in Christ Jesus' (Philippians 3:14). That was Paul's motto; is it ours? If Ruth's great pledge says anything, it tells us that for her everything had become new. Nothing was going to be the same again.

I want you to notice how everything had become new for Ruth. Hers were tears of joy that told she had found something new and lasting, something precious and enduring that she could never live without.

So Orpah had emotions without depth. Ruth had emotions that welled up from the depth of her commitment to God. If all we have is emotionalism, then there will be little substance to our faith. But if our religion is emotionless, we can genuinely question whether it is real. The last thing I want is a Gospel that will not reach into the depths of my being and stir my affections and my emotions. There is something wrong if we can preach the orthodoxy of the Bible in an unfeeling, a hard or cold-hearted way. The Gospel is not to be admired like some cold statue in a museum somewhere. When God blesses the gospel to us, Christ becomes so real that he stirs these kindled emotions in the depths of our soul, and enables us to say, 'Old things have passed away, all things have become new' (2 Corinthians 5:17).

I want you to note, first, that *Ruth found a new path for her feet*. 'Don't ask me to go back, or to return from following you, for where you go, I will go.' She had a completely new direction for her life. In the land of Moab she had wandered and strayed in paths of false religion and under the prophets of false gods. She had gone from one religious experience to another, yet her life was empty. Now she knows that there is peace and blessing, contentment and joy to be found by walking in God's way. She testifies that she has found a better path for her feet, and that is where she is going to walk. It may take her to territories that are unknown and to difficulties and experiences that she has never dreamt of, but that is the road she is going to walk. It may be, to use the words of the poet Robert Browning, the road 'less travelled by', but it makes all the difference.

The Bible tells us that there is a way that seems right to a man, but the end of it is death (Proverbs 14:12). Jesus puts it otherwise when he says that there is a broad way that leads to destruction and many, many people are walking that road (Matthew 7:13). That broad way is so wide that it will embrace many a religion and many a religious experience. Yet at the end of it there is a lost eternity.

There is, however, another road which leads to eternal life. Jesus says that it is narrow, and to be entered by the 'strait gate'. Perhaps you have read Dr Martyn Lloyd-Jones' exposition of the Sermon on the Mount; if so, you will recall his illustration of the strait gate. He says that it is like the turnstile going into a large stadium. Perhaps you have gone to watch a game of football, or rugby, and you have had to go into a stadium, which is usually filled with hundreds of people. Lloyd-Jones says, 'How did they get in there?' They went in through the turnstiles, *one by one*, a stream of people entering the stadium individually one at a time. So it must be with us. We must make our personal decision to leave Moab and to go to Bethlehem. No-one can make that decision for us, or enter the kingdom of God on our behalf. The decision to accept Christ is an individual one, and the decision to reject Christ is also an individual one.

There is something else. When you are going through a turnstile you can't take cases and heavy baggage with you; you've got to leave it all behind and just take the minimum in with you if you want to join the crowd. All this is implied in what Jesus says about the strait gate which leads to the narrow way. Look into glory; look at that innumerable crowd of people who are in Heaven. John tells us that it's a multitude that no man can number; we cannot even begin to reckon the number of people that God is going to have in the glory of Heaven with him throughout all eternity, but how did they get there? They went by the narrow way, and they went in through the strait gate, one by one. Every single one of them entered individually, shed their burden at that gate, every one of them died to self there, took up the cross there, washed their robes in the blood of the lamb there and went in.

Do you know what it is to walk that way? Do you know what it is for the Gospel to become so absolutely personal and so absolutely individualistic that you know God is speaking to you heart to heart? Is there baggage that you have to shed, things that are getting in the way, things that are preventing you from closing in with Jesus and finding peace with God? It is not worth taking all that baggage down that broad way; that leads to Hell, but I tell you this: it is worth shedding it all to get in at the straight gate, because the narrow way leads to life. Ruth wanted to walk the way that Naomi was walking. Naomi was blazing a trail that Ruth wanted to follow. The writer to the Hebrews says much the same thing in Hebrews 6:12: 'we are following those who through faith and patience inherit the promises.'

Perhaps you are saying to yourself, 'I would love to be a Christian. I would love to go in at that gate and walk that narrow path but I just cannot do it. What will people think about me? What will others say about me? I have too much to lose, too much to give up.' Just lift up your eyes to those who've walked that way before you. Remember that many of those with whom you will be travelling have walked that road before you; perhaps they are in your home, in your community, following the Lord for many, many years. Walk after them! Walk with them! They have come to know the faithfullness of God in their own lives, they love the Saviour with hearts that have been tested through the furnace of affliction. They have been tried in God's crucible; God has brought them through testing times in their experience and they are following Jesus.

Think too of all those Christians who are now no longer in this world. Remember those believers that God brought into your life, with whom you spoke and conversed and walked along life's way. They've been taken out of this world into a better one. They are now at their destination, at the haven they desired to see. A point came when God said about them, 'I want to take them home with myself' and God took them away, and you are left with their memory. Covet the way that they walked! Seek the Christ that they found along the way, and take up the cross and follow the same Saviour, so that you will find the same peace and blessing for your own soul.

Secondly, Ruth had found *a new place in which to dwell*. 'Where you stay, I will stay.' She wanted to share a home with Naomi, to be where Naomi was, to waken where Naomi wakened and to put down her head where Naomi put down her head.

There is a saying that home is where the heart is, and Ruth's heart was in Naomi's home, as she sought God's blessing on her life. That is why she wanted to be with Naomi, because she knew that she would find the Lord in Naomi's company. It is a clear biblical doctrine that God dwells with his people; and if we want to find him, and dwell with him, it is to the gathering of his people that we ought to go. We will find Jehovah in the company of his own. Ruth knew that she would find the Saviour in the presence of his own church, and she knew that wherever one believer is, there is the church.

If there has been an interest kindled in our heart for the things of God, we will find God in the company of his people. Ruth wants the God of the covenant, and she will find him with his covenant people. It is in the company of the sheep that she will find the shepherd. In the home of Naomi, Ruth knows she will find the blessing of God, because the blessing of God is on the habitation of the righteous (Proverbs 3:33).

I think that this is a fundamental principle, yet it is often undervalued. Too many Christians have neglected the church and its ordinances. Perhaps they feel that they have good reason to. Many denominations have failed God's people, by becoming so sidetracked from the Gospel that what they offer is little more than sentiment and tradition. Yet it is important to emphasise the biblical nature of the church; the church is where God's people are. And where God's people are is where God himself is. That was, after all, at the heart of the covenant (cf. 1 Kings 6:13, 2 Corinthians 6:16). In our search after God, and in our walk with him, we must join ourselves with his people, and dwell with them. We shall discover God in their fellowship, in their worship and in their company. It is a sin to 'forsake the assembly' (Hebrews 10:25), and, equally, a blessing to make use of it.

Many of you will be able to testify to this very truth. In your search for God, perhaps there were certain homes and churches which you knew to be blessed of God. We need many homes and churches like that, where the grace of God is at work, where the word of God is foundational, where the glory of God is sought, where parents and children and families worship God together and where the presence of the Lord is. Just as in the days of the early New Testament church, it would turn our world upside down (Acts 17:6) to have such places as these in our communities.

Thirdly, Ruth had *a new people to love.* 'Your people shall be my people.' She said that from the depths of her heart, even though she didn't even know these people of whom she spoke! Yet she loved them still. Her heart went out to the people of God, the people of the covenant. She was a stranger to them, and at this point they were strangers to her. She was literally 'alienated from the commonwealth of Israel' (Ephesians 2:12). Yet her heart went out to the people of God.

John, that great apostle of love, tells us we know that we have passed from death to life because we love the brethren (1 John 3:14). He describes the change that grace has wrought in the hearts and lives of God's people as a resurrection, a passing from death to life. But it is a resurrection which bears the fruit of love. So the order of *experience* is new birth first, then love for the brothers and sisters. John is using the order of *reason*; we find that we love the people of God and we reason from that fact to the fact of the new birth. Such a love is not found, John implies, among those who are still spiritually dead.

Do we love God's people? Ruth did. She thought of them, and wanted a place among them. I think there are times when perhaps Christians may find little evidence in their lives that they are Christians except this one great distinguishing feature: they know they love the people of God. God loves his own people. He loves them with a burning affection that began when there was no beginning, before the foundation of the world. God loved them from all eternity, and he has given every sinner who came through that straight gate a love for them too.

Christ loved them with such an intense devotion and zeal that he gave his life for them. He loved his church so much that he gave himself in order to redeem that church and present it as a glorious church without spot or wrinkle or any such thing. Those who love him say with Ruth, 'Your people shall be my people.'

Fourthly, Ruth had *a new peace in her heart*. 'Your God shall be my God.' God cannot be ours, until we are at peace with him. The Bible tells us that without God and without grace we are wandering like sheep, we've gone astray to our own way (Isaiah 53:6). But more than that, we are at enmity against the shepherd. We hate him, and he is our enemy. But Jesus Christ, the shepherd of the sheep (Hebrews 13:20) became the substitutionary lamb, who stood as the just one in the place of the unjust (1 Peter 3:18). The reason he did that was in order to bring together these two parties who were formerly at war with each other. That is the basis for the biblical doctrine of *reconciliation*. Jesus came and he preached peace. When he comes into the hearts and lives of those whom the Father gave him, and for whom he died, he removes the enmity, and he replaces war with peace. This peace belongs only to those who have been justified by faith, through the Lord Jesus Christ (Romans 5:1). They will have many times and experiences in their lives when there will be trouble and affliction, but there is no war between themselves and their God anymore. They have been reconciled by the death of God's son (Romans 5:10), they are at one with him, they have fellowship with him, He is their God.

The question is not whether we believe in God; it is whether we can say that 'this God is my God'. The essence of the covenant of God's grace is a person-to-person relationship: 'I will be their God and they shall be my people' (Genesis 17:7; Jeremiah 31:33). It was into that covenant bond that Ruth desired to enter, and it was in the God of the covenant that she found peace. That's what gave her peace in the depths of her soul, in her heart and in her life. God was her God.

Fifthly, Ruth found *a new prospect for her life*. 'Where you die will I die, and there will I be buried.' Not even death held fear for her anymore. The prospect of dying and being buried was not a terror to her. She was more afraid of Moab than of death. She knew that when the time came for her to die, she, like Naomi, would rest her head on the pillow of all of God's covenant promises and of covenant hope.

The Bible reminds us that it is a serious thing to die, but the Bible tells us that all of God's people have a hope in their death. When Paul knew that the hour of his death was coming near, that soon he would have to close his eyes in death, he could say 'I know whom I've believed, and I am persuaded that he is able to keep what I have committed unto him against that day' (2 Timothy 1:12). That's the way to die! 'I know that my redeemer lives,' says Job, 'and even after my skin is destroyed, in my flesh, I will see God' (Job 19:25). John, on the Isle of Patmos, lifted up by the Spirit on the Lord's day to see the glory of Jesus Christ, looked into Heaven and saw the place that God had prepared for his people, where there was no more death and no more sorrow and no more sighing. These things had all passed away.

Have you got that prospect? It was said of the Puritans that because they knew how to die, they knew how to live. Let us remember that; it is only those who know how to die well, that know how to live well. It is only those who have sorted out the great interests of their soul that are able to say,

'Come life, come death, whatever is before me I know that I am safe in the hands of Christ.'

Ruth was walking a new path, going to a new place with love for a new people, a new peace in her heart, a new prospect before her. Even were she to be separated from Naomi, nothing would change her resolve. 'Even if death parts us, I'll go on.' Naomi said nothing more. There is a time to speak, a time to counsel, a time to advise, a time to give a word of encouragement, a time to give a word of consolation- but there is also a time to say nothing, because the matter between a soul and the Saviour is so personal. Martin Luther once said that religion was a matter of personal pronouns. It is about saying of Jesus 'MY Lord and MY God' (John 20:28). Do we know the power of the Gospel captivating our hearts, thrilling our souls, and leading us heavenwards in the sure knowledge that nothing in heaven or on earth, in the past, present or future, can separate us from the love of God in Christ (Romans 8:39)?

The arrival

Now the two of them went until they came to
Bethlehem … they came to Bethlehem at the beginning
of barley harvest. And Naomi had a kinsman of her
husband's, a man of great wealth, of the family of
Elimelech; his name was Boaz. Ruth 1:19–2:1

You will recall that at this point in the story of Ruth a momentous decision has been taken. Ruth, who was brought up in the land of Moab and in its religious customs and manners, has decided to throw in her lot with the people of God, and to follow Naomi to Bethlehem. Whenever the Gospel has a saving effect in the lives of men and women, it shows itself in a clear decision. We may rightly be very suspicious of decisionism, and the kind of evangelism and preaching that presses for—and even pressurises people into making—an immediate decision. There are many people who have gone forward in evangelistic campaigns who never followed Jesus in reality at all. No preacher, of course, can allow people to leave with the impression that there is no urgency to the claims of the Gospel; but neither dare we leave them imagining that a decision to 'come forward' is always the same as genuine conversion.

There is, however, no genuine conversion, without a decision. God's grace moves a man's heart and mind and will. The person who is the object of God's saving grace and in whose life God has done a glorious work makes a decision that changes the whole course of their life, just as Ruth did at this particular point. Although Naomi's words seemed to encourage her to go back to Moab, there was nothing that could persuade Ruth to do so. So we read these great words of Ruth 1:18, that 'when Naomi realised that Ruth was determined to go with her, she stopped urging her.' There's a time to speak and there's a time to be silent. Naomi has the wisdom to leave Ruth to the grace and leading of God. Ruth made her decision and she was

Chapter 6

determined and so we read 'the two women went on until they came to Bethlehem'.

Now the scene changes. At 1:22, Naomi and Ruth return to the Bethlehem that was left behind in verse one. The Bethlehem that had been subject to the ravages of famine at the beginning of the chapter is now ablaze with fields of wheat, and alive with the work of the harvest. Fields that had been barren when Naomi last looked on them, perhaps a dozen years before, are now shimmering, and waving with the corn that is now so plentiful under the blessing of God.

When Naomi and Ruth come to the gate of Bethlehem, suddenly all the city is 'stirred' about them. Perhaps the meaning is that the women of the city whose husbands were out working in the fields of the harvest saw this other woman coming; she looked vaguely familiar, yet if it was Naomi, she was a shadow of her former self, and the years had taken their toll. She'd gone out in the bloom of health; to use her own words, she'd gone out *full*, but now she's coming back a different person. The onlookers are not even sure if it is her. 'Is this Naomi?' they are asking.

Of course, they don't recognise Ruth, but they seem to remember the features of this woman who was once so attractive in her physique, and once so active with them around Bethlehem's streets and in Bethlehem's fields, now looking altogether different. One cannot come through the affliction and the pain that Naomi has endured without being affected by them. That is why she says to them, 'Do not call me Naomi. Call me Mara.' The name Naomi means 'pleasantness'. The name Mara means 'bitterness'. She felt, after all that had taken place in her life, that the sweetness had gone, and that bitterness had replaced it. From the plains and the paths of pleasantness, and from the ways of peace, she had travelled to the barren lands of bitterness. 'I went out full,' she says, 'and the Lord emptied me. Don't call me Naomi when God's hand has been so heavy against me.' With these words she comes back into Bethlehem, at the beginning of barley harvest.

In this great transition that takes Naomi and Ruth into the land of Bethlehem and into the fields of barley, we have an overview of Naomi's whole experience of grace. It's all here, and in these verses, at the close of Chapter One and at the beginning of Chapter Two, we have a commentary on the whole of Naomi's life.

A look at the Past

I want us to look first of all, at Naomi's past. We've traced many of the details that the Book of Ruth tells us about Naomi: how she went out with her husband Elimelech looking for plenty in the land of Moab and finding there only the bitterness of sin and of death. The prospect that took them away from the land of privilege and blessing to the land of idolatry and godlessness, yielded a sad return. At three graves in Moab, Naomi had learned this invariable rule of Biblical ethics: that the further you stray from God, the nearer to death you come. She has discovered that the wages of sin can only be death, and the gift of God that the people were enjoying in Bethlehem was life.

Life or death: that is the Gospel choice. It is brought before us at every stage of Biblical revelation. Moses says to the people, 'I've set before you life and death, blessing and cursing, choose life that you may live' (Deuteronomy 30:19). Jesus Christ says to us in the New Testament 'I am come that you might have life' (John 10: 10). In Jesus there is life, and his life is the light of men (John 1:4). But Jesus tells us that men love darkness rather than light, because their deeds are evil (John 3:19). The teaching of the Bible is the teaching of the two ways; and the great issue of the Gospel is whether we will walk the way of light and life, or the way of darkness and death. The same choice, the same contrast runs throughout the pages of Scripture, and presses itself upon us in the preaching of the Gospel. Are we going to close in with Christ and have the life and the blessing that are in him, or are we not?

There were many people at this particular time that traded their opportunities in the land of blessing and privilege and promise, for the empty dreams and broken promises of Moab. In actual fact, Moab is where the real famine was, and Naomi learned that to her bitter cost.

That is the condemnation under which this sinful world of ours is labouring. Perhaps you are labouring under it too. Maybe you have strayed far away from God, far away from his people, far away from fields that are full of covenant provision? If so, then the story of Naomi ought to encourage you, for it is the story of the whole Bible. It is the story of the Gospel of the grace of God, that those who were far off, are brought near by the blood of Christ (Ephesians 2:13). Naomi strayed far from God, far from covenant blessings, from covenant promises, from covenant opportunities, and she found bitterness in her soul as a result. The more distance we put between ourselves and the blessings and the privileges of the covenant, the more it will be that pleasantness will give way to bitterness in our lives. The Gospel is calling us to come to the God of the covenant, not to stray away from him.

Naomi had not only strayed from the God of the covenant, she'd been 'emptied' by the God of the covenant. When you look through the Bible and at the ways in which God deals with men and women, this one great issue stands out time and time again. In order for a man to enjoy the blessing of God, he needs to be emptied. He needs to be emptied of himself and of all his natural self-importance and his natural pride. That pride is what drives the wedge between himself and his God. Naomi says to us as she reflects on the way by which the Lord took her, 'God emptied me. I left Bethlehem with a fullness, and I am coming back with absolutely nothing.' She is to learn that only by having been emptied can she enjoy God's blessing in the fields of barley harvest. The emptiness in her soul is going to be the way to a greater discovery and experience of God's blessing and nearness.

I come back to the Lord's great words in the New Testament to all these religious adults who flocked around him, interested in what he had to say, in the propositions and the theology that he taught. He says to them, 'Unless you become like little children, you cannot enter the Kingdom of Heaven' (Matthew 18:3). Yet it is the most difficult thing in the world for a man to become like a child! Jesus is saying to us that if we are to enjoy the blessings of kingdom life, we need to be emptied of all these feelings of self-achievement and self-importance, to lose every vestige of the pride that is so inimical to our relationship with God. We carry round with us constantly this great sense of our own achievement, of what we've accomplished, and what we've done. God is saying to us that if we are to enter into the fields of blessing, we must first shed that load, and get rid of all that excess baggage that is weighing us down and keeping us back.

Here is Naomi, who is going to go on to know and enjoy so much, telling us here that God had to empty her. I wonder if you know anything of that great experience of soul-emptying and of heart-emptying, so that nothing matters at last but what you are in Christ and not what you are in yourself? Do you know anything of what it is to be stripped of all your self-righteousness, to be reckoned as nothing before God? Every sinner that has crossed this threshold, and has come into the great land of blessing and forgiveness has come through this door of self-emptying, self-abasement and self-awareness.

When we are born again, God makes everything new. He takes over. He has to demolish the old structure of our lives and reconstruct a new building. When a man is converted it is like a shop that is now under new management. The old shop is of no use for the purposes of the new manager. He has to demolish the old building and construct a new one that is suited to his purpose and fitted for his service. Naomi says now, 'That's what God did for me.'

So here is Naomi's testimony: she strayed from the God of the covenant, and has been emptied by God, but she also tells us that she has been *led* by him. 'God brought me home again'. That is her great testimony. The Lord took her home. The lostness of Moab has given way to the leading of God.

There are two names for God brought before us in these great verses. He is called the *Lord*, that is Jehovah, the sovereign God of the Covenant, and he is called the *Almighty*, the God who came to Abraham and said, 'I am the Lord God Almighty. Walk before me and be perfect' (Genesis 17:1). The name Jehovah reminds us of our obligation to him. The name Almighty reminds us of his grace to us, and here is Naomi singing the song of her God. 'I know,' she says, 'that I strayed from the will of this sovereign Jehovah, but the Almighty broke into my experience. He didn't leave me where I was; I unmade myself but He found me and he took me, and although he brought bitter things into my life, he took me back, back to the land of covenant blessing.'

Is that not the story of every man, woman and child who has ever found grace in the Gospel? 'I once was lost, but now am found, was blind but now I see.' Naomi acknowledges that she travelled long on sin's road and in sin's company, but grace found her and brought her home, and it is the story of every child of God who is able to say like Paul, 'I am what I am, by the grace of God' (1 Corinthians 15:10). And all because the Son of man came to seek and has saved that which was lost (Luke 19:10). Salvation came to the home of Zacchaeus, not because he sought the Lord (although he did), but because the Lord sought him. That Lord came right into his experience, and turned his world upside-down, and Zacchaeus goes on from that day saying, 'I've got a Saviour, who found me, and who saved me, and who's keeping me every day of my life.' Naomi's story is the same. 'He found me, and he took me and now he's brought me home'. The Gospel story is addressed to those who have wandered away from the paths of Jehovah, and it promises them the aid of the Almighty.

Naomi's Present

So here is Naomi, now entering Bethlehem. The fields that were once ravaged by famine are now full. The corn is plentiful. God has visited his people and given them bread. Naomi finds herself there, coming into the fields of Bethlehem, and into this place that is overflowing with the blessing of God, at the beginning of barley harvest, and she has her daughter-in-law with her. She is not returning home alone. She is returning home in the company of Ruth.

I think there is something quite beautiful and quite magnificent here, and that is this great emphasis on the sovereignty of God in salvation. Do you see how this is emphasised in 1:22? This is Ruth, the *Moabitess*, and the God who looked after Naomi and guided her is the God who did the unexpected and found Ruth. Not only so, but he also made Naomi a blessing to Ruth. Now Naomi is coming into Bethlehem in the company of her daughter-in-law. In the darkest of Naomi's hours, as well as in the most testing places of her life, God has been there with her, and one evidence of his grace is that the Bible says 'So Naomi returned *and Ruth the Moabitess her daughter-in-law with her!*'

Here, surely, is the rainbow of God's sovereign purpose shining in the blackness of Naomi's sky! She came to realise that every trial and every difficulty in the lives of God's children has God's blessing all around it. Sometimes it is near impossible to realise this, when the darkness is pressing in, and when the flood and the fire are so overwhelming. It is difficult then to say that God is working all these strands of experience together for good. It is easier to say with Naomi, 'this is bitter for me' than to say 'this is better for me'. Yet the story of Naomi reminds us that every step we take as believers is a step along the road of God's purposes. What a blessing to have this great assurance in our own lives!

It is only the Christian who is able to look at affliction that way. I suppose at last that it is one of the great tests of our Christian profession. It's so easy to make a profession when things are well, to sing 'Our God Reigns' when the winds are favourable and the sun is shining. By the still waters and the green pastures it is easy to sing 'The Lord is my Shepherd', but when a man in the furnace of affliction can say, 'God is my God and though he slay me, yet will I trust him' (Job 13:15), then there is living proof of real faith. It is there you have the acid test that this man is truly a child of God. It is easy to sing at the top of the mountain; but take a man into the valley, subject him to trials and temptations and testing times there—will this man still say then that God is his, and that he is God's? The Apostle Paul knew blessing in his life: he had assurance of God's presence, and blessing on his work as a preacher and evangelist. But he has also known trials and afflictions. What does he say about them? 'Our light affliction, which is but for a moment, works for us an exceeding great and eternal weight of glory' (2 Corinthians 4:17). If you were to take a pair of scales, the affliction on its own would weigh you down, but weighed against the weight of glory, the affliction is light!

The great shepherd psalm, Psalm 23, talks of leading by still waters, and feeding in green pastures, but it also talks of walks through the valley of the shadow of death. It talks of enemies and trials. These experiences do not belie the bond between the shepherd and the flock. He is their shepherd still. There is a song which says:

The God of the mountain is still God in the valley,
When things go wrong, he'll make them right;
And the God of the good times is still God in the bad times;
The God of the day is still God in the night.

That is how Naomi is here. She's been through her valleys of darkness. She's had her bad times. She's proved the faithfullness of God. If the presence of Ruth testifies to how far away from God Naomi went, it also testifies to how near to Naomi God came. Ruth the Moabitess is with her! The blessing of God is in her cup, along with the bitterness and along with the trial and along with the affliction—it's all been mixed together for good, as God promised.

Naomi's Future

But there is something here, I think, about Naomi's future too. Her past has been woven with a variety of threads, light and dark, a mixture of light and shadow; her present now gives evidence that the blessing of God has been on her life and has been with her up to this point. What of the future? What about the days to come? Well, God has made provision for her there too. 'Naomi had a kinsman (NIV: 'a relative on her husband's side') whose name was Boaz' (2:1). There was much that Naomi did not know at this particular time. She did not know what lay ahead or what life in Bethlehem would mean for her now.

At the beginning of Chapter Two we are reminded that God knew, and had already made the provision: there, in the fields of Bethlehem, there was a man who was going to be a means of blessing to these two women. God is running before Naomi and before Ruth. He is breaking up the way, preparing the way, and making sure that everything they need is ready. Isn't it so easy to fall into the pit of despair and depression simply because we cannot face tomorrow? Are we not reminded here that the God who holds us also holds the future, and he has already singled out Boaz, who is going to do Naomi good?

For every one of us who loves Jesus Christ, there is this great assurance. Much may be unknown to us, but God has already made the provision for all our tomorrows. He has already written the providence that will keep us and guide us in all that lies ahead. He has already appointed the means and the men by which blessing will come; he has already decided on the ways by which we will know his nearness and his favour—it's all there in his plan. 'Don't worry about tomorrow' (Matthew 6:34), says our Lord. Paul puts it like this: 'In everything with prayer and supplication and thanksgiving, make your requests known to God and the peace of God will keep you (Philippians 4:6–7). The God who kept his eye on Naomi has already got his eye on Boaz as a means of blessing and of provision.

Sometimes we become preoccupied to the point of depression with the future of the church, but God has already provided for the future of the church. We often become so preoccupied with our own personal immediate futures and yet we must learn that God has already made provision for our future. We become afraid of what we cannot see; yet God asks us to live by faith because he sees the end from the beginning. He's already got this man, this mighty man of wealth, of the family of Elimelech, marked out, and through him blessing will come to Naomi and to Ruth, and to the whole world.

That's the kind of God that we have: the God who runs before us and who says, 'wherever I take you, I have gone before; and wherever I lead you, I have already been, and whatever you experience I have already prepared what you need'. What a blessing to be safe in the hands of that God! Although we do not know what the future holds, we know who holds the future. If you are unconverted, I am asking you to come with all your cares and all your burdens and your anxieties, and I am asking you to bring them to the God of the covenant. Let him empty you of all that you ever thought you were, so that he'll fill you with a blessing that overflows.

If you know him personally, I am asking you to go forward in the strength of God, the Lord. He can see much further than you can, and he has already been ahead, paving the way, preparing the road, and blazing the trail to glory. Did he not say 'I go to prepare a place for you' (John 14:2)? Does he not call us his kept ones (1 Peter 1:5)? When we come into his fields there will be provision for us—'enough and to spare'—and his grace will be as our days. Our God does not change. What he was for Naomi and Ruth, he will be for us. The answer to the cares of our past, present and future is to be found in the one who is the great 'I AM', the Lord Almighty, whose name is Jesus.

The gleaning

And her mother-in-law said to her, 'Where have you gleaned today? And where did you work? Blessed be the one who took notice of you.' So she told her mother-in-law with whom she had worked and said, 'The man's name with whom I worked today is Boaz'. Ruth 2:19

The events that are recorded for us in the Book of Ruth revolve around harvest time and the gathering in of the grain. It was because of a poor harvest that Elimelech and Naomi and their sons had left Bethlehem in the land of Judah to come into the country of Moab. It was because God had sent bread that Naomi returned. The time of their return is described in Chapter One as the beginning of the harvest.

There were at least two immediate problems that needed to be dealt with when Ruth and Naomi came to Bethlehem. The first was where they were going to stay: the question of their accommodation. The Bible doesn't tell us where they stayed but it is clear that they found a home where both of them were able to live temporarily. The second problem was food and provision. The second chapter of Ruth shows how wonderfully God fed them and looked after them in their new home.

In Chapter Two we are introduced to another person: a rich and influential man who was related to the family of Elimelech, whose name was Boaz. So much is Boaz going to take a central role in the events that unfold in this great book, that you would be forgiven for renaming this book the 'Book of Boaz'. From this point onwards he becomes absolutely crucial and central to all the events that are to unfold in the life of Ruth. But it is not the Book of Boaz; it is the Book of Ruth, because it tells us of God's special provision for Ruth *through* Boaz, through this mighty man of wealth. Boaz was a man to whom Naomi was related only through her late husband, and yet that connection was enough to secure provision.

It was because of this family connection that a door opened, and Ruth was able to go into the fields of Boaz and glean ears of corn. We read in this chapter about the special provision which Boaz made for her, and how Boaz counselled Ruth to stay in his field. 'Do not go to any other field', he said. 'Don't go from here. Stay here by my maidens. Let your eyes be on the field that they reap, and go after them. I have charged the young men that they shall not touch you' (2:8–9). Ruth recognises the grace of God and the bounteous provision of God before her here in the fields of Boaz. So when she comes home at the end of the day, with a bag full of corn that she is able to make into flour and then into bread, Naomi asks her, 'Where have you gleaned today?' in the knowledge that the blessing of God has accompanied Ruth.

This chapter tells us a very interesting thing about Ruth: she occupies a two-fold position at this point. We are told in verse twelve of this chapter that she has a place *under the wings of God*. We know from Chapter One and the events that unfolded in Moab and on the road to Bethlehem that Ruth had indeed turned her back on Moab with all its gods and idols, to put her trust in the one living and true God. She had come to trust under the wings of the Lord God of Israel, and because she was under the wings of Jehovah, she was also *gleaning in the fields of Boaz.*

It is important that we see the link between these two things. There is an intimate connection between them. Under the wings of Jehovah she is enjoying a provision that is given to her in the fields of Boaz. God has brought her to put her trust personally in himself, in Jehovah, the Lord God of the covenant. God shows that his blessing is upon Ruth by making this rich provision to her when she comes into these particular fields to glean and to gather corn. Under the wings of God and in the fields of Boaz is where Ruth's provision is found.

When a person comes to trust personally in the living and the true God for salvation, that person will be found looking for spiritual bread. Just as trust in Jehovah made a gleaner and a gatherer of Ruth, and left her seeking and searching in the fields of Boaz, so it makes a gleaner and a seeker of us too. If we come to trust in the Lord, we will search. We will seek and search for Christ, for the living bread which came down from Heaven. Our trust is in the God of the covenant, and the sustenance that our soul needs is to be found in a particular place. 'Search the Scriptures', Jesus counsels us in John 5:39. These are the fields of Boaz to us—the Word of God, the preaching of the Gospel, the fellowship of God's people.

Jesus taught as much in his parables. What is the Kingdom of Heaven? It is like a man sowing seed, with different results (Matthew 13:1–23); it is like a field where good seed is sown, but tares grow up among the wheat (Matthew 13:24–30); it is like mustard seed growing in a field (Matthew 13:31–2). Peter talks of God's people being 'born again, not of corruptible seed but incorruptible' (1 Peter 1:23) which Peter identifies as the word of God, and contrasts with the grass of the field which withers as soon as it is grown. God is a planter! Indeed, this is an important image in the word of God, from the Old Testament picture of the believer's soul as a 'well-watered garden' (Isaiah 58:11; Jeremiah 31:12), to Jesus' image of himself as the true vine, and his people branches in the vine (John 15:1–8). The fields of Boaz are an apt metaphor for the work of salvation in the hearts and lives of God's people.

What is the church? It is where sinners gather in Gospel fields in order to glean corn for bread! The church is nothing but a gathering of poor, empty, needy sinners, gleaning in the fields of God's provision in order that their souls might be fed, because their trust is under the wings of Jehovah. That is why God's people search the Scriptures: it is because they are trusting in Jesus Christ, sheltering under the wings of Jehovah and seeking him in the Bible.

What is the place and purpose of Boaz in the Book of Ruth? He is the one who will undertake the duties of *kinsman-redeemer* on behalf of Ruth. We shall explore the implications of this later; but the essential meaning of this role is that he is the one by whom Ruth may be provided for. There is a Boaz in the Bible, a kinsman-redeemer, who has opened for sinners the vast provision of Gospel blessing. He enables us and invites us to come, and to put our trust in the Lord, by gleaning in his fields. I know there are people who say 'I can be a Christian without going to church, without going to a prayer meeting, and without having fellowship with any of the Lord's people,' but God has joined these two things together intimately in the experience of his people. Those who are truly trusting under Christ's wings are gleaning in Christ's fields. Those who are truly seeking the Lord will find shelter under the covering of the wings of the Lord God of Israel. There is an intimate connection between the gleaning of which 2:3 speaks, and the refuge of which 2:12 speaks.

So the question that Naomi put to Ruth, when she came back this first evening to her home is as relevant and pertinent for us as it was for Ruth when she was asked it. Where do we glean? Where have we been gathering today? What does going to church, reading the Bible, singing the praises of God, mean for us? Is it a sign that we are trusting under the wings of Jehovah? Our profession to be trusting in God is seen in our diligence in gleaning in his field.

As we look at this day of gleaning in Ruth's experience, there are three things that we need to note: barriers, bundles, and blessings.

Barriers in the fields of Boaz

I want to talk first of all about barriers, because I think that there was one special barrier before Ruth at this particular point. She had come out of the land of Moab, following Naomi. Her heart was changed; the interests that she once had, she no longer had. Things that once occupied her attention, suddenly were of no consequence. Things that were once all-important now had a very secondary, insignificant place in her thinking. All that she wanted was to come into the inheritance of the people of God, to join with them, and to know the reality of what she expressed when she said to Naomi, 'Your people shall be my people; your God, my God.'

However, there was one great stumbling block in the way, and unless it was dealt with she could never have a place among God's people. It was in *the very law of God itself*, and it focussed on the fact that she was a Moabitess.

I think, in fact, that the writer of the Book of Ruth is at pains to remind us of this problem. In this immediate context Ruth is not simply called Ruth. Time and again the maiden-stranger is given her full description as 'Ruth the Moabitess'. You find her described in this way in 1:22 and 2:2, and then in 2:6 as 'the young girl from Moab'. Why is this fact emphasised? Simply because it represents the one great thing that could prevent Ruth from coming into the inheritance of God's people.

God had spelt out very clearly in his law, in Deuteronomy 23:3, that 'a

Moabite or an Ammonite shall not come in to the congregation of the Lord, not to the tenth generation.' Just as the law of God had said that his people should not go to Moab, so it said that they should not welcome any from Moab into their community. It was God's infallible, authoritative, unchanging, holy, sovereign law that now pointed the finger at Ruth and said 'You can't come into the inheritance of God's people. You are a stranger to the God of the covenant. By nature, you have no claim on the God of the covenant.' So there is a small clause in God's holy law that is large enough to prevent Ruth from coming in to enjoy what she wants to enjoy among the people of God. She wants in, but God says she cannot come in.

To borrow Paul's statement in Romans 8:3, there was something here that the law could not do, because it was weak through Ruth's flesh. The law was incapable of admitting Ruth into the company of God's people. The reason for that was not because there was anything wrong with the law, but simply because of what Ruth was by her very nature. The law of God— the law which was holy and just and good (Romans 7:12)—was weakened by Ruth's flesh. All her natural ties were with Moab. Moab was in her blood, and therein lay the problem.

In essence, that is always the problem. Our way back to Paradise has been blocked by the fiery sword of God's absolute justice and holiness (Genesis 3:24). Paul's argument in the New Testament is not that we can try our very best and perhaps find peace with God. His argument is that no matter what we do, how we act, the way we think—everything about us is tainted by sin. The flaming sword is turning every way, and every aspect of our lives is found to be at fault. There is none righteous, and there is nothing about you or me that is righteous. The problem is not in God, nor is it in the law of God, nor is it in the nature of God. The problem lies with our own nature, corrupted and tainted as it is because of our estrangement from God.

That is what Paul is arguing in Romans 8. There is something that the law cannot do, because it is weak *through our flesh*. The law itself has no inherent weakness. Perfect lawkeeping is the basis for eternal life. God related to man at the outset on the basis of such a covenant, which theology subsequently called a covenant of works. Although some have questioned the legitimacy of that form of description, it summarises the arrangement of the Garden of Eden. Indeed, both before and after the Fall, God's grace to man is mediated through law, and specifically through law-keeping. Adam, who represented the whole human race, was told that on the basis of his doing some things and not doing other things he would enjoy unbroken fellowship with God. He would know life in its fullness, but instead of being confirmed in a state of purity and of life, he sinned, and, because he was the representative of the human race, the whole human race sinned too.

The result is that we are all in Ruth's position. Our sinful nature is what prevents us enjoying full communion with God. Our sin prevents our access into God's presence. We are sinners by nature as well as by practice and have more of Moab in us than we care to imagine. God says of sinners that they cannot come into the same tent as him. That's how the psalmist puts it in Psalm 24:3, 'Who may stand in God's holy place?' Who can share a tent with God? David is alluding there to the Hebrew emphasis, I think, on hospitality: give someone a place in your home, or a seat at your table, and you have established a bond. But who can share table with God? Who can dwell in his tabernacle?

The same psalm answers the question: 'only those whose hands and hearts are pure, who do not worship idols and never tell lies' (Psalm 24:4). How can we judge whether our actions are acceptable or not? Only by weighing them and assessing them in the light of the law of God, which is not simply a set of his standards—it is also a revelation of his character. Those who share space with him must be like him, and the reality is that God's law stands before us, condemning us, driving us away, closing the door, building a barrier. It says that we cannot have life because we are sinners, because we are 'carnally minded' and therefore at enmity with God (cf. Romans 8:6; 1 Corinthians 2:14).

Our problem is that Moab is in our very thinking, in our whole life and interests, and in the motivation for all we do. To be 'carnally minded' is to be spiritually dead, and those who are spiritually dead cannot come into the inheritance of the people of God. What is Ruth to do? She had said to Naomi, 'I want this more than anything else,' but God's law says to her 'You cannot have it. You cannot have it because you are a Moabitess.' This uncompromising law of God places this stricture before her. Judah is a no-go area for a Moabitess.

Chapter 7

The glory of God's grace shines through his law. That is something that we often fail to emphasise. We regard God's law as something bleak and dismal, something negative and disabling, something that hinders and curtails. Yet the law is as much a revelation of grace as of holiness, of love as of justice. The same law which forbade Ruth from entering the congregation of the Lord also made provision for her to come in!

Is that not wonderful? The same God who, in his law, declares Ruth's inability, also, *in the same law*, opens a door of grace for her. While Deuteronomy 23 spells out the reasons why she might be excluded from the community of Israel, Deuteronomy 24 opens a way for her to come in. Deuteronomy 24 contains the laws regulating the harvest. There God said to his people: 'when you go to harvest your corn, don't cut the corners of the field. Keep them for the stranger, for the fatherless, and for the widow. If you drop anything when you're gathering in the corn, don't pick it up. It's for the stranger, for the fatherless, for the widow. When you come to take in the grapes, and you shake off the grapes from the branches of the tree and the grapes fall into your basket and there are some left on, don't pluck them off. They are for the stranger, for the fatherless, for the widow' (see Deuteronomy 24:19–22). The reason this law is incorporated into the deuteronomic code is in order that God's people will remember that they too were once strangers, and that by his grace God brought them out of Egypt's slavery and into Canaan's liberty.

The amazing thing is that Ruth qualified on these three counts! She was a stranger in Bethlehem, she was fatherless in Bethlehem, and she was a widow in Bethlehem. I think it is one of the most glorious things in this great Book of Ruth, that the very law which prevented her access, was the same law which provided her access. It is the law that says there is a provision here for strangers, for the fatherless, for the widow. God remembers the poor and the outcast, and he reaches out to them to bring them into his covenant.

Paul's teaching in the New Testament is that the same law whose effect was weakened by our disobedience, so that we could not enjoy the blessings of God's salvation, has been fulfilled for us by Jesus Christ. God, in his grace, reaches out to those who have no natural right to his blessing, and no natural access to his throne. There is no breach of law, no injustice at all, in the way God saves. By nature we are excluded from the covenant community, but in the death of Christ God has upheld his law and put honour on it. By grace, our debt has been paid and our needs have been met. Jesus has taken our place, bearing our sins in his own body on the tree. He, in the words of 2 Corinthians 5:21, was made sin for us that we might be made the righteousness of God in him. Hugh Martin, the great Scottish theologian of a past day, described this as 'imputation and counter-imputation'—our sins were reckoned to Christ's account, and his righteousness to ours. He is regarded by God in the light of our law-breaking, and we are regarded by God in the light of his law-keeping. The same law that keeps us out has also provided a way of bringing us in. Listen to this: 'The law of Moses could not save us, because of our sinful nature. But God put into effect a different plan to save us. He sent his own Son in a human body like ours, except that ours are sinful. God destroyed sin's control over us by giving his Son as a sacrifice for our sins. He did this so that the requirement of the law would be fully accomplished for us who no longer follow our sinful nature but instead follow the Spirit' (Romans 8:3–4, NLT).

So, for Ruth, barred as she was from the covenant community because of her natural ties to Moab, God found a way. Grace opened the door. His salvation was for the impoverished, the outcast, the stranger; they could glean. That's all Ruth could do. So she did what she could, and she gleaned. So it is with us. The law of God says to us that by nature we are alienated from God and strangers to the commonwealth of Israel and the covenants of promise (Ephesians 2:12), but the same Bible that condemns us as sinners and says that we have no right of access to God, tells us that there is something here for sinners. Why should Ruth perish outside when a door of opportunity beckons? Why should sinners die in their sins when a door of Gospel opportunity invites them to make use of what Christ offers as the way to God?

There is something else. Gleaning was a *harvest* thing. You could not glean at sowing time, or at growing time, or at watering time. You could only glean at *reaping* time. You could only glean when the work of the harvest was ready. The law that provided access for Ruth did so on the basis of a finished work! All the sowing had been done, all the watering, all the tending, all the looking after the field, that work was now over. This was the end. It was on the basis of a finished work that Ruth was able to come into the inheritance of the people of God and realise her dream of making Naomi's people her own.

The Gospel offers eternal life to us on exactly the same basis—on the basis of a finished work. The seed has fallen into the ground and died; it is now bearing much fruit (John 12:24). As Isaiah put it long ago, the Messiah is to see of the travail of his soul (53:11). His death was not in vain. The work was planned in eternity, executed in time, and completed on the cross. There is a finished work.

When I come to the cross, that is what I am going to find there—a work completed. The man of sorrows has laid down his life for sinners, and because of his great, finished work, there is now an abundance of harvest, bread enough and to spare for strangers to glean. Although the condemning voice of God's law says to us 'You cannot get in', the sweet, winsome, warm sounds of grace come to us through the Gospel and says there is a finished work that opens the gate to sinners. That burning, turning sword has plunged into the heart of Jesus Christ, and his blood can cleanse from all sin. God does not ask us to understand great doctrines, or to grasp deep theology—he asks us to come in our need and to glean in his field. The provision is there, for the stranger, the fatherless and the widow. Christ did not come to call the righteous, but sinners to repentance (Matthew 9:13). Blood is shed, and hope is offered. Death claims Christ and life flows to us. He thirsts that we might drink. He dies alone that we might glean. He is the bread of life come down from Heaven, and the Gospel points us to Calvary and says, 'Come and glean'. Grace overcomes the barriers. Mercy has triumphed over judgement (James 2:13).

Bundles in the fields of Boaz

Now I also want to think about *bundles*. Ruth discovered something very precious when she went into the fields; Boaz knew her, and had already seen her, and, unknown to Ruth, was making enquiry about her.

In fact, we have a very beautiful picture of Boaz here in these fields in Bethlehem. Did you ever notice for example that no other name is mentioned in these fields, but the name of Boaz? There were many servants there, many reapers, many people, working and employed in these fields, but all we know is the name of the overseer, the name of Boaz himself. Is it not the same with the Gospel? The only name worth knowing is the name of the redeemer, the name of Jesus Christ. In all the industry of the church of Jesus Christ of the world, his name is supreme. Who is the Creator of Heaven and earth, the King of the Ages, the Jehovah of the Old Testament, the great 'I am' of Moses and the Messiah of the prophets? He is the one of whom the angel said 'Call his name Jesus' (Matthew 1:21). Paul said, 'We preach not ourselves, but Jesus Christ the Lord' (2 Corinthians 4:5). Is it not a characteristic of Paul's ministry that he is constantly striving to draw a veil over himself so that men will be left hearing of one name? His great purpose in proclaiming the Gospel is that men will be left looking to the one person who is central to the whole Gospel of grace, Jesus Christ, the only Saviour of sinners.

The only name in these fields worth knowing was the name of Boaz, but we ought also to note how Boaz comes close to his reapers. He comes from Bethlehem and into the field where his reapers are gathering the harvest. He speaks with them as he walks among them and he says 'The Lord be with you,' and they answer 'The Lord bless you' (2:4).

Remember what John saw of Jesus in the Book of Revelation: he saw Jesus, and juxtaposed with the *description* of his glory is the statement of his *position*: he was bright as the sun for brilliance, yet he was standing in the middle of the golden lampstands (Revelation 1:12–16). These lampstands represented the church, and the Lord of glory was standing there. That is how it is in the church of Jesus Christ: Christ is with his people, and he is walking with his people, and he is talking to them; and he is blessing his people, and his people are blessing him. There is a personal contact, a personal communion. Boaz does not act like a distant overseer, an absentee landlord. No, for Ruth he is 'a very present help in trouble' (Psalm 46:1)

Then the narrative tells us about *the personal interest Boaz takes in Ruth*. He knows all about her. He counsels her not to glean in another field, but to stay in his. That is what Jesus is like. He takes a personal interest in us. He says, 'I have called you by your name; you are mine' (Isaiah 43:1). His is the only field worth staying in. It is in the Gospel that we will find what our souls need. It is from him that we will obtain what our lives lack. Wherever the Gospel is preached, where the people of God gather to love him and to feel his name, Jesus says, is the place where we ought to be.

Unknown to Ruth, Boaz had spoken to his reapers and had commanded them to give her special protection and special care; he had also told them to let handfuls of corn drop on purpose for Ruth to pick up. The law did not require that of him. All the law required of him was that he did not cut down the corn in the corners of the field, and if any corn dropped accidentally when it was being reaped, it was to be left on the ground. However, grace always abounds extravagantly. So Boaz says to his reapers: 'let handfuls fall on purpose'.

Why was that? First, these bundles fell *because of the abundance of the harvest*. Where once there had been famine, now there was plenty, so that Boaz could spare bundle upon bundle for Ruth to gather. The whole was his: the whole field, and all the corn. Bundles were nothing to Boaz, but what a difference a bundle made to Ruth! She had nothing at all. She had no claim on the field, no claim on the ground or the corn or the food, but out of this tremendous richness, handfuls dropped for her.

It is one of the great teachings of the Gospel that there is enough in Christ to satisfy the needs of every and any sinner who comes to him. There is an absolute and unconditional guarantee that whatever our need is, and whatever our condition and situation may be, there is a fullness in Jesus to meet the needs of all. Does John not tell us that it is out of his *fullness* that we received, and grace for grace (John 1:16)? Does not Paul say that his God is able to supply *all* our need out of the riches of his glory by Christ (Philippians 4:19)? I am saying that the fields of Boaz are full to overflowing, while the fields of Moab offered nothing but loneliness and heartache and grief. What a contrast between the fields of Moab and the fields of Boaz! Ruth buried a husband in the fields of Moab, because sin always ends in death. The fields of Moab gave her a place to bury her dead, but the fields of Boaz overflowed with abundance, giving her all that she needed, and more. These bundles of corn were the signs of an extraordinarily plenteous harvest. The Christ we preach, the Christ who is offered in the Gospel, is extraordinarily full for poor, needy sinners to come to him.

These bundles were also *signs of a personal interest* and love that Boaz had for Ruth. He said about her, 'Let her glean, and look after her, and let her come and sit with my maidens so that she'll have enough and be sufficed and leave. Let handfuls of corn fall on purpose so that she'll glean, and she'll take them home.' There was a personal interest here, and every time Ruth picked up a bundle, she could say 'This was for me.' It was not just one or two ears of corn that she obtained, but a handful dropped on purpose every time, with the precise intention that she would pick them up.

How often has God done that in our experience? Perhaps there were times when we were feeling at our lowest, and we did not know where to go. Just then, it seemed as if God went out of his way to make specific provision for our need, dropping bundles of blessing on purpose for us. Maybe we heard an appropriate sermon or read a book or heard a relevant word, and discovered that the Scriptures were tailored to our very situation. In the quiet of our soul, we rejoiced and said, 'God went out of his way to do this for me!'

In times of sorrow, God gave us comfort; in times of darkness, light; in times of weakness, strength. There were times when at the point of our very need, God dropped a Gospel promise our way, his word took wings and it flew right into our heart and into our soul bringing peace.

What a tragedy it would have been had Ruth left these bundles lying on the ground! She had her own responsibilities to attend to. Boaz was the provider, but Ruth was the gleaner. I wonder if it's possible for us sometimes to leave God's bundles of promise and blessing lying on the ground? To have the word of God there beside us, with all its glorious sufficiency and fullness, and yet never to make use of the opportunities and blessings God sends your way. Let's make sure we are diligent gleaners in the fields of our Jesus-Boaz!

Blessings in the fields of Boaz

For Ruth, there were barriers that were overcome, bundles that were dropped on purpose for her to pick up, and there were blessings that she enjoyed in the fields of Boaz. Let me mention just two of these.

Ruth, first, enjoyed the blessing of *sufficient food*. We are told in 2:18 that Ruth came home to her mother-in-law, Naomi, and she was 'sufficed'.

That is a great word: it means that she wanted nothing more, and she needed nothing more, and she lacked nothing. She had the blessing of sufficient food, because she took the corn with her and she measured it out, beat it and made flour from it. With the flour she made bread, and she ate the bread, and there was enough to satisfy her when she and Naomi sat down for their evening meal.

That is God's promise—the promise of absolute sufficiency. God's people may go into eternity with very little of this world's provision. Many, many saints have traversed the long path of life's pilgrimage with little or nothing of this world's riches, honours, fame or prosperity, but they had all that they needed because they had the Lord. They were 'sufficed'.

Let me put it this way. God has only one Saviour, and God is satisfied with the one Saviour that he has. I think that faith in the soul of a sinner is the echo of God's satisfaction with Christ. The soul that trusts is the soul that says, 'I am pleased with Jesus too.' He is all-sufficient, nothing can be added to him and we dare not detract anything from him. All that we need and long for is in Christ. Ruth gathered what she found, and made use of what she gathered.

She also had the blessing of *a daily provision*. Naomi could ask her 'Where did you glean *today*?' At the end of the day she could say 'Right up to this moment the Lord has helped' (cf. 1 Samuel 7:12). That great word of confidence and thanksgiving looks forward to help for another day, and grace for another day, and bread enough for another day. Even though we do not know what tomorrow may bring, this we do know: that his grace is sufficient for us every single day!

Our lives are full of change and uncertainty, but here is the one great blessing for all who come to Jesus: the promise of a daily supply of grace. There is daily provision in the fields of Boaz for those who will glean there. So where have you gleaned today? Are you feeding on the finest wheat, trusting your soul to the only saviour? Do you know anything about feeding off the table of the Gospel and the bread of life? Let the fields of Moab go, since the fields of Boaz beckon!

The light

Naomi said to Ruth her daughter-in-law, 'It is good, my daughter, that you go out with his young women, and that people do not meet you in any other field.' So she stayed close by the young women of Boaz, to glean until the end of barley harvest and wheat harvest; and she dwelt with her mother-in-law'. Ruth 2:22–23

When Ruth came home, at the end of her first day in the fields of Boaz, Naomi said to her, 'Where have you gleaned today?' She was then able to tell her mother-in-law of all the wonderful provision that God made for her. God had been going before her, opening the way for her, preparing the path that was to bring her into the fellowship and circle of God's covenant people. Through the marvellous grace and kindness of Boaz, blessings flowed into the life of Ruth. For us, too, there is a Christ offering himself to us in all his glorious fullness, and his invitation is extended to us to make use of him.

I want us in this chapter to spend a little time thinking about the conversation between Ruth and Naomi. I believe that it was crucial, as a directive and incentive to Ruth at this point in her life. We are told that Naomi said three things to Ruth. First, in 2:20, she blessed the Lord for Boaz—that was a word of *rejoicing*. Then, again in 2:20, Naomi describes the relationship in which Boaz stands to them—that was a word of *revelation*. Finally, in 2:22, Naomi speaks of Ruth's relationship to the other gleaners, and I am going to suggest that that was a word of *rebuke* to Ruth.

There is, I think, an important principle emerging here. It is that the speaking of Naomi is so crucial to the development of the story. What a wise woman she is! Just as at 1:18 Naomi's silence was so critical, now her speaking becomes pivotal. There is a time to speak, and a time to be silent.

This is a time for speaking—Ruth needs direction, and with the gentle leading of Naomi she will be guided into the next stage of her journey. Ruth needs counsel. She needs to hear what Naomi has to say, which is a word from the Lord, a word which is born out of her knowledge and her experience.

Paul's classic statement of the inspiration of the Bible in 2 Timothy 3:16 not only tells us that all Scripture is inspired by God, but goes on to say that it is profitable for us, for our instruction in righteousness, for our counsel, for our guidance, so that the people of God will be equipped for every good work. This emphasis on the centrality of the Bible is one of the hallmarks of evangelicalism. It is the word we need, and it is sufficient for every situation and circumstance. Naomi's words to Ruth were carefully chosen, and timeously given. They were a word from Heaven to Ruth's soul, and were a light to guide her on her journey.

Part of what this teaches us is the importance of fellowship. Although it is sometimes important to have specialist interest groups in our churches (young people's fellowships, senior citizen groups etc), there is also a great benefit to be had through integration and togetherness. Ruth learns much from Naomi's counsel; Naomi is enriched by Ruth's presence, and by the evident blessing of God upon her life. Perhaps what we need is less segregation and more togetherness in our churches!

A Word of Rejoicing

The first of Naomi's words to Ruth expressed her gratitude to God for the attention Boaz has given them. 'May the Lord bless him!' is what she says of Boaz. The word 'bless' has not been often on the lips of Naomi. She has talked of emptiness—but now she is aware of fullness. She has talked of bitterness, but now she can talk of blessedness. When Naomi hears that it is in *Boaz's* fields Ruth has been gleaning, she breaks out with this great note, this anthem of rejoicing and praise of the Lord, 'The Lord bless him! He has not stopped showing his kindness to the living and the dead.' Not all that long before this there had been another word on the lips of Naomi. When she came to Bethlehem and the people that saw her were moved, they could hardly recognise her weakened form coming back from Moab after such a long absence of at least ten years. Now she is back, after a decade, and the whole city is moved by Naomi's situation and she says, 'Don't call me Naomi, call me Mara because the Almighty hath dealt very bitterly with me' (1:20). You see the word on her lips at that point was the word 'bitter'.

Naomi has seen all these handfuls of corn that Ruth is gleaning and her voice has changed, her word is different, her whole attitude is different. Everything about her is different. She has moved from bitterness to blessedness, from saying that the hand of God has been against her to saying now that the hand of God is with her. She said first of all 'God has stood against me', now she is saying, 'God is for me'. In that provision that Ruth brought home this evening Naomi sees God's unfailing kindness, his covenant love, his absolute faithfullness to his covenant people and promise.

Although Naomi drifted far away from him, God remained the faithful God of Naomi. He has taken her out of bitterness and into blessedness. She went to Moab in order to get food with Elimelech, her husband, but her plans were overthrown, and she says as she comes back 'bitterness, bitterness'. However, now she sees this great provision, now there is bread in the home, now God has been so evidently going before her, she is saying, 'blessedness, blessedness.'

Is that not what God does for men and women? That is the joy he gives. That is the note of rejoicing that he plants in the hearts of men and women who have strayed far away from him, and in his grace he has brought them back in to the bond of his covenant, back into the fellowship and to the circle of his own people. They too have made this great transition from bitterness to blessedness.

Here is the great lesson of the unchanging faithful God of the covenant—he is able to lift us out of bitterness and he is able to give us blessedness. He is able to transform the night into day, to scatter the shadows of all of these feelings and to come into our lives with the brightness of the noon-day sun. Do you remember how the psalmist put it so vividly? 'You have turned for me my mourning into dancing; you have put off my sackcloth and clothed me with gladness' (Psalm 30:11). Remember what we read about the disciples in the New Testament: 'Then were the disciples glad, when they saw the Lord' (John 20:20). The moment they saw him, it transformed their whole outlook and their praises began and their hearts were caught up in the thrill of knowing him and having him there.

Does it move your heart to rejoice with Naomi, to see the Lord's gracious hand in the experiences of your life? Does it move your heart to hear Christ extolled and exalted every time the Gospel is preached? Does it thrill you to read about all that he has done and all that he is as the bread of life come down from Heaven? If we can look into the Bible, and read about the Saviour and his dying there for sinners and remain unmoved, there is something radically wrong with us. God can change situations, and can fill us with rejoicing and blessedness. Is that not what Psalm 126 is full of? 'When God turned the captivity of Zion, we were like men that dreamed, our mouths were filled with laughter because God had done great things for us' (Psalm 126:1).

Have you any reason to praise the Lord today? Having seen him at work in your life, and having discovered what he is in himself and what he has done for sinners and has promised to do, do you have any reason to sing his glorious praises? To exalt his name and to call him blessed? Do you know anything about that? Remember that the work of Heaven is a work of praise. The moment a door in Heaven is open for John in the Isle of Patmos to see what is happening on the other side, immediately he hears singing. He hears an anthem being sung. He hears a name being exalted, with heavenly music and celestial singing, he hears the choirs of angels and the spirits of justified men made perfect, singing the praises of him that loved them and washed them from their sins in his blood. Do you know anything of that singing?

God's people have something to sing about. I have belonged all my life to a psalm-singing denomination, although I have had the great privilege of preaching and worshipping in a variety of churches whose approach to worship is different to mine. I respect all those who take the Bible as the rule for their worship, even if they apply it in ways different to me, but I take exception to the highbrow, highly choreographed worship style which insists I should be jumping for joy with a laugh on my face every time I sing God's praises. The psalms of the Bible do not insist on me being happy every time I praise God! Let's remember that! Sometimes they reflect the fact that my soul might be filled with sadness and melancholy. The glorious thing is that even when I don't feel like singing, I can recognise God's goodness and acknowledge his love. Bible joy is not dependent on circumstances, but transcends them, and enables us to lift our head above the waves and to bless the Lord from the depths of our soul.

When the Bible talks about God's people as being *blessed*, it is not necessarily describing a state of emotional joy. I question whether the word 'blessed' in Scripture should be translated as 'happy'. Happiness is a subjective, emotional condition—blessedness is an objective state. If I am blessed, it does not matter how I may be feeling, and I can bless the Lord even from the depths of my sorrow and need. After all, what the Bible says is that the joy of the Lord is our *strength* (Nehemiah 8:10), and even in our lowest moments we can experience God's blessing upon us and his strength fortifying us against all difficulties.

I think that is how Naomi is. She has had her share of heartache and tears, but there is joy in her heart. There is melancholy, but there is also melody. Her life had been so changed by the grace of God that she couldn't but shout out when Ruth came home, 'The Lord bless him!' There is rejoicing on the lips of Naomi. May God keep us from a religion that does not move us to rejoice! From a religion that does not capture us with the thrill and the glory and the joy of God's salvation! I think that is what Naomi is experiencing here at this point, a transition from bitterness to blessing. Her rejoicing is the measure of what God is able to do in one human life.

A Word of Revelation

Naomi then told Ruth that the man with whom she had worked was related to them: 'This man is a relative of ours, one of our near kinsmen' (2:20). This is obviously a very important thing to Naomi because she repeats it in the following chapter. In 3:2 she says to Ruth, 'Now Boaz, whose young women you were with, is he not our kinsman?'

Naomi sees the significance of this fact: that the man in whose fields Ruth went to glean, was Boaz, their close relative. There were family ties here, which were important as a basis for future security. The Bible does not spell out for us what the relationship was, but it was close enough to give Naomi hope.

The important question to clarify is this: what hope did the fact of Boaz's being a relative give to Naomi? I think it gave her a two-fold hope that was based on the provisions of God's law, particularly the laws we read about in Deuteronomy 25 and Leviticus 25. One law stated that if a family lost their father through death, a close relative, (a brother, or in some cases another relative) could bring up the children and continue the family name within the household (Deuteronomy 25:5ff). This included the brother or close relative marrying the widow and having children with her. The law also included a proviso that if the close relative did not wish to do this, the widow could sue him before the elders of the city.

There was another law that stated if a man lost his property, then another kinsman could redeem it and buy it back (Leviticus 25:23–34). This law is based on a two-fold principle: first, that the land belonged to Jehovah (no-one could claim absolute ownership), and second, that restoration was an expression of grace. The idea of redemption had already been fundamental in Israel's history—the release from Egypt was an act of redemption (Exodus 15:13). In terms of land ownership, God's law made provision for lost land to be restored, either through the payment of a redemption price, or in the Year of the Jubilee.

Although the legal situation behind the Book of Ruth is complex, it is clear that here we have a mingling of these two laws, and the themes of continuation of the family name, and restoration of the family property. We see, as the Book unfolds, that the story of Ruth is one of redemption by a near relative. Boaz is going to do two things: he is going to fulfil the law in respect of marriage and in respect of property. He will play the part and fulfil the obligations of a kinsman-redeemer, by which he will continue the name of Elimelech, and see to the restoration of the land.

One of the most significant commentaries on the Book of Ruth is the mention of Boaz in the genealogy of our Lord (Matthew 1:5). Not only in the immediate story of Ruth, but also in the 'bigger' story of God's salvation, Boaz is going to play a primary and pivotal role. Indeed, precisely *because* of his involvement with Ruth he will have a significant role in the unfolding purposes of God's grace. But there is something else: because of the way in which Boaz will fulfil the two-fold law regarding family and property, Ruth is going to find a way in to the covenant people of God through marriage.

That is why Naomi is so thrilled by this tremendous provision. Ruth had said to Naomi in 2:2, 'Please let me go to the field and glean heads of grain after him in whose sight I might find favour.' Was that only this morning? Ruth did not know where she was going when she set off. All that the Bible says in 2:3 is that '*she happened* to come to the part of the field belonging to Boaz …'. What a wonderful coincidence! I believe in coincidence; it just means two events (two *incidents*) happening at the same time. I do not, however, believe in *mere* coincidence, but in *measured* coincidence. I believe in God's ordering of every event and his working out his purposes in the events of this life and in the coincidences of this life. In God's providence, when two things happen together at the same time, it is not without a reason. It was a coincidence that Ruth found herself gleaning in the fields of Boaz, but it was not a mere coincidence. It was not an accident. It was not without a design. God brought her into that field, and now Naomi is explaining to her the significance of it all. The man is a close relative. He is able to undertake the duties of a kinsman-redeemer. He can continue the family name, and secure the interests of the family inheritance. He is able to do for them the things that they cannot do for themselves, Naomi is saying to her daughter-in-law. There are issues here, she is revealing to Ruth, that are beyond their own capacity and ability, but this man is the answer.

This is precisely the point at which the Book of Ruth becomes so full of Christ and his Gospel. There is a redeemer who can do for us what we cannot do for ourselves. We take Christ's lead and search the Scriptures because they testify of him—and we find him here, in this Book of Ruth, portrayed for us in the work and in the ability of Boaz. Can we imagine Christ unfolding himself out of the Old Testament to the disciples on the road to Emmaus and not stopping in his exposition at the Book of Ruth? Can we doubt that he drew attention to the laws which Boaz alone could fulfil—laws that could ensure the continuance of the line of his people and guarantee the security of their inheritance? Only one man could do it—the man who was related to them and acceptable in terms of the law's standards.

Jesus Christ is brought before us on the pages of the Gospel as precisely such a man. He, and he alone, can do things for us that we cannot do for ourselves. He is able to undertake our interests for us when our own hands are tied. There are limits to our ability and our power, but there is a Redeemer, Jesus, God's own Son. The glory of the Gospel revelation is that the one in whose fields we glean in the Gospel, shares our blood-line as Mediator, the God-man, Christ Jesus.

The glory of Christ's redeeming work lies in the fact that he did not take to himself the nature of angels, but he took on him the seed of Abraham (Hebrews 2:16). The glory of his redemptive work lies in the fact that the Son of Man was made a little lower than the angels. It was fitting that in all points he should be made like his brethren (Hebrews 2:17). In order to save the lost sons and daughters of Adam, Christ had to 'destroy him who had the power of death, that is the devil, and release those who through fear of death were all their lifetime subject to bondage' (Hebrews 2:14–15). Who is the devil? He is represented as the enemy of God, the angel who wished to be God and who set his sights on occupying the throne of the universe. He is portrayed in Hebrews as holding in fear and bondage those who have followed him and who are slaves to sin. The death of Christ was many things, among which it was an assault on the devil's kingdom, power and lordship in human life.

The teaching of Hebrews 2 is that in order to destroy the power of the devil, Jesus did not take on the nature of angels—to destroy an angel he had to become a man! He took our nature to himself, and was found in fashion as a man. It is the close proximity of Jesus to those whom he determined to save that is the basis upon which an effective redemption can be accomplished.

Just as the glory of Boaz for Ruth and Naomi lay in the closeness of the relationship that bound him to them, the glory of Christ for us lies in the nearness of his relationship to us. There is one who is near of kin to us. Love compelled the godhead, as one poet put it, to wear frail flesh and blood. Jesus stands before us as an able and a competent Saviour, and his ability and his competence and his power to save arise out of the fact that things came to be true about him that had not always been so. The second person of the godhead, the delight of the Father, the God who has no point of origin, the God who is eternal and unchangeable, possessing all the glories that belong to the absolute supreme being, the Son of God now, in addition to all of these, has taken bone of our bone and flesh of our flesh. He remains an eternally divine person, but he has two natures: he is God and he is Man. The one nature has not extinguished the other. His man-ness has not extinguished his God-ness; his God-ness has not extinguished his man-ness. They are not intermingled into one nature, they are not confused, the boundaries between them are clear. But they are united together forever in his one person. That is why he can save. That is why he is able to undertake all the duties of a Redeemer and do for sinners what they cannot do for themselves.

Hebrews 2:17 presses this to its great climax and to its great consummation. Why did Jesus become like his brethren? So that he will be a merciful and faithful High Priest. In things pertaining to God, man and law, in every issue of our life, Jesus is able to perform the duties of Priestly Redeemer because he was made like his people. He took the likeness of those whom he intended to save, lived a life for them in the world and took their place when he died to be punished for their sins. He rose with power in their likeness. At the right-hand of God, in their likeness, he intercedes on their behalf. And every one of these heirs of salvation has only one Saviour, who is near of kin to every one of them.

I want to ask how near is Jesus to me personally? Hebrews 2:18 tells me, 'He suffered being tempted; He is able to aid those that are tempted.' The one who suffered is able to help. Or, to use the language of the King James Version, the *sufferer* is the *succourer*. The one that endured the cross and despised the shame is able to give strength and grace to all of his people; he is that near to them. He is a close relative. That means that he understands perfectly everything that I may be experiencing, enduring and suffering, and is able to give grace and help to those who stand in need of strength and grace and help. He can identify with weakness on the part of his people. He can feel their pain and understand their need. The God-man is the one who can truly stand by us and help us every step of the way.

A Word of Rebuke

I am going to suggest that there is a third thing on the lips of Naomi and it is a word of *rebuke*. In 2:21 Ruth added the following information: 'He also said to me, "You shall stay close by my young men until they have finished all my harvest."' The striking thing about that was Boaz had not said this to

Ruth at all. Boaz had said to Ruth, 'Stay by my *maidens.*' In reference to the young men, Boaz had said to Ruth 'I have commanded the young men not to go near you. They'll not harm you.' He had not counselled her to stay close to the young men.

In fact Naomi, who was not in the fields of Boaz at all, hears what is being said. This is how Naomi answers Ruth, 'It is good, my daughter, that you go out *with the young women,* and that people do not meet you in any other field.' It is not with the young *men* that Ruth ought to remain, but with the young *women.* What seems to be stressed in 2:21 is that Ruth misrepresented the words of Boaz. Was this the *Moabitess* in her speaking? Is there a signal here that there are still sinful tendencies that need to be overcome?

Even when God, by his grace, changes our status from sinners under condemnation to sinners justified, and makes all things new for us, there remains in our hearts a world of corruption which needs to be dealt with and overcome. That is what the doctrine of *sanctification* is about—it is about our lifestyle, our desires and our motives matching our status before God. I wonder if, in Ruth's statement, there was something of the sin that remains in all of God's people, coming here to the surface and calling forth a tender rebuke from Naomi. Boaz did not, in fact, tell Ruth to stay close to his young men. So Naomi gently corrects her. 'Stay,' she says to Ruth, 'with his young women.'

The interesting thing is that the closing words of Chapter Two make it clear that Ruth heard, took, and acted on, Naomi's counsel. In 2:23 we read that until the harvest was ended, Ruth 'stayed close by the *young women* of Boaz'. For all that the Book of Ruth tells the romantic story of a young woman of faith, it also tells a realistic story. Ruth was open to temptation as we all are. It takes a lot of courage, grace and strength to resist temptation. Sometimes we fall into temptation, only to be torn apart by remorse and sorrow for what we do. What a blessing it is that God, in Christ, covers our every need, and cleanses from every stain.

We do not read that Ruth sinned, but I do think we read that a door of temptation was opening. Then she hears the wise words of Naomi, directing her to retain her purity and integrity in Boaz's fields. The church is not free from imperfections and sins. Indeed, there are some people who are all too ready to point the finger at the church for her faults and inconsistencies, not one of which is justifiable or excusable. For that reason, there is a great encouragement for us in the Bible, because the Christians of the word of God, were, as Elijah is described in James 5:17, men and women with the same (sinful) nature as ours. That takes us back to the fact of Jesus being made a perfect high priest by taking our nature: he knows the reality of temptation and is able to help those who are tempted. It was not without reason that his baptism was followed by six weeks of intense temptation in the wilderness. He can understand and follow and sympathise with—and help—those of his people who descend so quickly from the mountain tops of blessing and assurance to the valleys of temptation and sin.

Sometimes God allows us to fall into these very sins and temptations. The story of Naomi herself shows us that, and also shows us that God is able to use the hard lessons of our lives to show us our weakness and sin, that we might all the more lean on him and put our trust in him. It was the same with Peter, when he denied three times that he knew the Lord. Hard as the lesson was, and hard as the long nights of sorrow and tears afterwards were, Peter was of benefit to the church following his experience of temptation, sin and repentance. His sin emptied him of all the self-reliance and independence which had led him to deny Christ. He came to see himself as nothing, as one who needed to be kept by God's grace and power (1 Peter 1:3).

So Ruth continued gleaning, and working, as God blessed his people with harvest and with bread. While walking the path of integrity, holiness and obedience, Ruth found blessing. There is no blessing to be found along the path of compromise, sin and disobedience. But there is blessing to be found in the path of God's will. May we all learn to walk that road, and enjoy the bounty and fullness of God's blessing!

The quest

And Boaz said, Who are you? And she answered, I am
Ruth your handmaid ... You are a near kinsman.
Ruth 3:9

The first chapter of Ruth tells a story of wasted years. It is a chapter
filled with tears and full of disappointments. These
disappointments came because of a departure from the law of God.
Instead of obeying God's voice in revelation and in providence, and
repenting of their sin, Elimelech and his family went to Moab, forsook God
and looked for help and provision in the land of sin and in idolatry. And the
wages of sin, as always, for them was death.

Chapter Two spoke of working days, in which Ruth went to glean in the
fields of Boaz. The law that closed a door of access also opened the door to
that communion. There was a law that allowed strangers to glean and to
share in the blessings of God's provision. God, through Boaz, made
provision for Ruth. So she came and gleaned in the fields of Boaz.

Chapter Four is going to be a chapter of wedding joys, but first there
must be a night of seeking and of waiting. In many ways Chapter Three is
the most difficult to understand; yet it is essential to this story and to the
revelation of God's salvation. The chapter, we must note, is precipitated
and set in motion by one great concern on the part of Naomi for Ruth. 'My
daughter,' she says in verse one, 'shall I not seek security for you, that it may
be well with you?' That is the one great issue that is burning in the mind and
in the heart of Naomi. The goodness of God has been so evident; the
blessing of God has been so bountiful; the grace of God has been so
conspicuous and so real. But Naomi knows—and this issue burns in her
heart—that Ruth is still a stranger in the land. Naomi's great concern is
that she will have 'security'.

The word that is translated 'security' in verse one, really means 'rest',
and it takes with it the idea of being settled and established. Though Ruth

gained by gleaning, it was not enough. She needed confidence and assurance that she had a place among God's people. That is the 'rest' that Naomi wants for Ruth, and she knows that if and when Ruth gets that rest, it will be well with her. There will then be no more uncertainty about her future, no more shadows over her life. The past will then have been gone and dealt with. The clothes of mourning that she wears as a widow can then finally be put away, and all that she has been carrying with her—the burdens that she took home from Moab, and all the tears and the loss and the grief that Moab ever meant for Ruth—will then have been dealt with decisively, definitively and finally. Ruth will have a place among God's covenant people. That is what sets these strange, intriguing events of Chapter Three in motion.

This is the fundamental issue that lies at the very heart of the Gospel. The Bible comes to us in the words of the Gospel and in the words of Naomi, 'Shall I not seek rest for you that it may be well with you?' The only thing that can give us security and the assurance of God's blessing and of eternal life is to find the rest that there is in Jesus Christ. Jesus himself uses that very word when he speaks to the Jews of his day. 'All you that labour and are heavy laden, come unto me and I will give you rest' (Matthew 11:28). The kind of rest that Jesus gives the longing soul is a rest that brings with it fullness and security and pardon; it's a rest that washes away all the burdens of the past. It's a rest that deals finally and definitively with all that we ever did and all that we ever were that came short of the glory of God. The peace that Jesus gives comes with the promise of eternal security for the man or the woman who sets his trust in the Lord Jesus Christ.

Let me put it another way. The world has its own promises of security, of fulfilment, and of peace. The world promises us peace on certain conditions, saying to us that if we get this or that, or if we do this or have that, it will be well with us. That is the kind of security the world offers: a satisfaction confined to the experience of certain pleasures, the possession of material things, or the knowledge that comes from learning and from education. But it is an elusive dream, as Ecclesiastes 2:13–18 testifies. How many people have lived for these very things? Yet their lives ended up in ruins. How many of the great achievers of our modern age have found real peace in their lives? They have raked in millions of troubles along with their millions of pounds! The world is littered with broken dreams, broken homes and broken lives, all of which remind us that there is no rest outside of Jesus Christ.

The great issue of this Bible is that our souls will find rest, and there is only one place where real, lasting security may be found. It has been put magnificently in the opening words of the Heidelberg Catechism: *What is your only comfort in life and death? Answer: That I am not my own, but belong with body and soul, both in life and in death, to my faithful Saviour Jesus Christ. He has fully paid for all my sins with his precious blood, and has set me free from all the power of the devil. He also preserves me in such a way that without the will of my heavenly Father not a hair can fall from my head; indeed, all things must work together for my salvation. Therefore, by his Holy Spirit He also assures me of eternal life and makes me heartily willing and ready from now on to live for him.*

That is a security that the world cannot give us, and that the world cannot steal from us. In that assurance, there is rest for our souls and security for our lives. Whatever may come our way, there will be rest and peace for us in the knowledge that we belong to Jesus Christ. So it was a great blessing for Ruth that Naomi was burdened for her welfare and security.

Twice the same question is asked of Ruth in the course of this chapter. In verse 9, Boaz asks Ruth on the threshing-floor, 'Who are you?', and in verse 16 Naomi puts the same question to Ruth. Boaz can be forgiven for not recognising the woman who had crept in to lie at his feet at midnight, but Naomi obviously was not asking about Ruth's identity. Instead, she was asking about how the midnight meeting had gone. The repetition of the same phrase, however, is significant, and reminds us of the fact that this encounter with Boaz caused a momentous change in Ruth's relation to Boaz, and, consequently, her own personal situation. Commentators have pointed out the contrast between these two meetings between Boaz and Ruth, the first in the fields of harvest, the second at the threshing-floor; the first accidental, the second deliberate; the first by day, the second by night; the first in public, the second in secret; the first for purposes of work, the second for purposes of marriage. The midnight confrontation was clearly momentous in its significance. It was also a very necessary meeting; the whole purpose of this meeting was that Ruth would have security. And Ruth found the security for three reasons.

Ruth came to the right person

She found rest first of all because Naomi directed her to the right person. Naomi reminded Ruth of the kinship of Boaz. 'Is not Boaz a kinsman of ours?' This was highlighted at the close of Chapter Two. It is a reminder to us that the whole redemptive work of Jesus Christ is effective for our salvation because Jesus has identified himself, in his nature, in his life and in his death, with the sinners that he saves. He took our nature. He is able to stand in the breach between God and men because he is the God-man. All that is true about God is true about him. All that is true about man, apart from sin, is true about him. There is no other God but Jesus and there is no other God-man. Jesus is our redeemer because he is the God-man. He is a Saviour because of his nearness of kin.

Just as Peter could say of Jesus 'To whom shall we go but to you?' (John 6:68), so Naomi can say to Ruth 'To whom shall you go but to Boaz?' This whole momentous, singular issue of her rest and security hinges upon her relationship to one person: not to Naomi, but to Boaz. The promise of Ruth's security lies in the uniqueness of Boaz, in precisely the same way that the promise of our rest and security lie in the person and work of the Lord Jesus Christ. Ruth, therefore, had to come to this particular person.

Ruth came to the right place

Boaz, then, was the one who could change Ruth's whole life, but if he was to do so, Ruth had to go to see him at a particular place. Naomi asks Ruth to wash herself, put clean clothing on and go down to the *threshing-floor*. It was the end of the harvest, and time for threshing the corn, for separating the kernel from the husk, separating what was inside and valuable from what was outside and unnecessary. Threshing depended to a large extent on the breeze; the sieve was used to separate the wheat from the chaff by tossing the corn into the air and over the sieve. The breeze would carry the chaff away and leave the wheat. The threshing time, therefore, was a time of separation at the end of the harvest.

It was also a time for festivity. A great deal of energy was expended at harvest time. Once it was gathered in, responsibilities were over, workers could relax, and there would be a party. Naomi knew that after the festivities of the threshing, Boaz would be at the threshing-floor, and Ruth could go to him there.

In the Bible, the threshing-floor is a very significant place. It's the place where the corn is sifted, and where the husk and the kernel, the wheat and the chaff are separated from one another. It's the place where what has been gathered can be separated. Then, what is of use can be kept and made into food, and what is of no use can be discarded, or used as fuel. Throughout the Old Testament there are times when the threshing-floor becomes the place where God deals finally and climactically with men and women.

For example, you will recall that on one occasion David was tempted to number the people of Israel. God had told him not to do so, but David yielded to the temptation and numbered them. God told David that what he had done was wrong; it was a sin, and it required God's chastening hand. In his grace, however, God gave David three choices: three years of famine, three months of war or three days of pestilence. David was at the threshing-floor of Ornan when God came to him and said, 'David, you've got to decide what you want'. David cast himself upon the mercy of God and chose the three days of pestilence, which Israel then endured. The threshing-floor was the place where God finally and climactically dealt with David and the sins of the people. The interesting thing was that the site of God's judgement and climactic dealing with David's sin was the very place where the Temple was going to be built. In another generation Solomon's Temple was built on the very spot of the threshing-floor of Ornan (see 2 Chronicles 3:1) where God dealt finally and definitively with David.

The same was true of Gideon. God came to Gideon and called him to be a judge over Israel. Gideon refused to entertain the thought and said, 'No, I'm the least of my father's house and my family is not great in Israel.' Here was a man wrestling with a call of God in his life, and what is he doing? *He is threshing wheat* (Judges 6:11), and he is doing it secretly, so that the Midianites will not steal the wheat from them. Here it is again: at the threshing-floor God separates Gideon, winnows away all his self-interest and all that is a barrier between Gideon and his service for God. So the threshing-floor becomes the place where God says, 'Gideon, you must follow me, and you must do my will and you must obey me.' The threshing-floor becomes the place where the scene is set for the deliverance of Israel out of the hand of Midian.

Or think of Peter. At one of the most climactic points of his life Peter was on a threshing-floor: the threshing-floor of Satan, who has a place where he sifts and where he tests, where he tries the mettle of the people of God. Christ said to Peter, 'Satan has asked to sift you as wheat' (Luke 22:31). There are places and times and experiences in the people of God where God allows them to go to Satan's threshing-floor, where they are tested. God allows them for a time to be in the Devil's sieve. Someone has said that it is better to be in the Devil's sieve than in the Devil's cradle. Jesus wants Peter to be a minister to his brethren—to comfort and encourage them after the resurrection. For Peter, the best preparation for ministry is on that spiritual threshing-floor, where all the self-confidence and self-reliance of Peter has to be sifted away.

Indeed, the final judgement is represented in exactly this way. When the nations are gathered before him and God sends the angels to gather his elect from all the corners of the earth, it will be like the reapers gathering in the corn from the field. The wheat and the tares that grew together till the time of harvest, will all be brought to God's threshing-floor, and he will separate chaff from wheat (cf Matthew 3:12; 13:30). There are many who have nothing more than an external profession of religion with no internal reality. But God says 'This is of no use to me' and at his threshing-floor of judgement God will separate the sham from the real. The wicked are like chaff which winds drive to and fro, whereas the righteous will stand in the judgement (Psalm 1:5–6).

Do you see—the threshing-floor is the place of decision; it's the place where God deals definitively with men and women, the place where God enters into final resolution with his own people. And the threshing-floor of Boaz was to be the place where Ruth would find the peace and the security and the rest for which her soul cried out.

For us, who by nature have no security before God, who are without God and without hope in the world, God has a place where he finally resolves the issues that affect our relationship with him. There is a threshing-floor to which God asks us to come, a place where God deals definitely and finally with every sinner who comes to him.

Where is this threshing-floor? Where else but at the cross of Jesus? It is there that God's judgement is poured out on his Son. It is there Christ is made the curse. It is there that sin is dealt with—blood is shed, and Christ endures the judgement on behalf of his people. There is separation, testing and judgement. Christ says 'My God, my God, why have you forsaken me?' (Psalm 22:1; Matthew 27:46)—he becomes the one who is cast out, in order that we might be brought near to him. God's judgement on his Son is in order that a final resolution of man's sin problem will be effected. The reason Jesus is made the curse is that we might have forgiveness and justification. In the Gospel, God asks us to come to the threshing-floor of Calvary. That is the place where God is able to deal finally and definitively with all our past, able to wash away every sin and every stain and 'all unrighteousness' (1 John 1:9). So at that cross, Christ asks us 'Who are you?' and deals with us personally and effectively. Justice is satisfied. Judgement becomes the basis for mercy, and mercy is expressed in the willingness of the Son to become the substitute and to bear our sins.

Naomi directs Ruth to go to the man who can redeem her. If she is to have security she must go to Boaz. If it is to be well with our soul, we too must go to the man who alone can redeem. But where is he to be found? It is interesting that Naomi gives three explicit directions to Ruth about where she will find the man who can redeem.

She says to Ruth first of all, *'Mark the place where he lies.'* At the end of the harvest, Boaz was at the threshing-floor. Naomi asks Ruth to note that place. Does the Bible not say the same to us about about our Redeemer? It asks us to mark the place where he lies. It asks us to come to the infallible and inerrant pages of Scripture if our soul is going to find peace and forgiveness and satisfaction, and there we can mark out and trace out in the word of God, the place where the redeemer lies.

We can note where he lies as an infant in the manger, dependent on the care of his mother to feed him and to clothe him and to look after him. This is the second person of the Godhead. He has entered into our nature, and he has come into the stream of human history. He has come from the outside and he is lying there as a child in the manger. Love has taken him this great distance to Bethlehem's manger.

We must also mark out where he lies in death on the cross. We take note of where he goes, where he has his final place, where he is seen before the eyes of men conspicuous in his death, watched by thousands as the spectacle of their scorn, and ridiculed at Calvary's cross. He does not have a quiet screened-off bed in the corner of a hospital ward. He does not have a place where he is surrounded by the warmth of his family and friends. His place of death is full of mocking and scorn. He is there as an object of comedy; he is there to be looked at; he is there to be spat upon and to be laughed at. Mark out where he lies, dying and dead, as the Saviour of Calvary.

Then trace where he lies in the cold of the tomb, sealed there and guarded there; his body is put there, handled so lovingly by these people who were secret disciples until their service calls them. Then out of their closets come Nicodemus and Joseph to do what they can for Jesus while there is still time. Joseph gives him his tomb, and his arms carry him, to the grave. There Jesus lies, in his state of humiliation, continuing under the power of death for a little time. There he is 'tasting death', in the words of Hebrews, grappling with death, taking the sting out of death.

Just as Ruth needed to mark the place where Boaz lay, we too need to mark where our Redeemer lies. We cannot know salvation, or peace, or security, until we have seen him bowing under the weight of the great work of salvation, reaching down to a world of need, coming to the cross of Calvary, and ultimately entering into the grave itself. If we are to come to him, we must come to him there.

Then, secondly, Naomi said to Ruth, *'uncover his feet'*. 'Mark the place where he shall lie, and go in, and uncover his feet'. That's the place for Ruth—at the feet of her kinsman-redeemer. The Gospel bids us do the same. We too must uncover the feet of the redeemer-Jesus. We can trace the path that these feet have trodden. We realise that this redeemer came purposely into this world in order to save. That was not a work that was thrust upon him in the years of his maturity or adulthood—it was a work that was given to him before the dawning of the ages. He came into the world walking the path of God's will and obedience to Jehovah. At the age of twelve he knew that he was about his father's business. At the age of thirty he said to the world, 'This is the father's will which sent me that of all that he has given me, I should lose none' (John 6:37–39).

As the shadows lengthen over the life of the Saviour and the cross comes nearer, Mary (another New Testament Ruth) comes to Jesus, and anoints him, and washes his feet. In fact, it is interesting that the three times we meet Mary in the New Testament, she is found at the feet of Jesus. When she entertains Jesus in her home, she sits at his feet to hear his word (Luke 10:39). When Lazarus dies, she falls at Jesus' feet (John 11:32) to unburden herself following the death of her brother. Then on Passover week she anoints Jesus' feet with the precious ointment (John 12:3). Mary has learned the value of coming to Jesus' feet. She can learn there, and weep there, and worship and serve there, and her anointing of his feet is so significant. More than the disciples themselves, she has learned that he is going to the cross. His hands and feet are to be pierced because of the sins of men and women in order that sins might be forgiven. His body will not be available for anointing afterwards, so Mary anoints his feet for burial beforehand. She has learned the secret of peace—the peace that comes from the Saviour who will die on her behalf.

Listen to him when he rises with triumph over death and over the grave, and he appears to the disciples and says to them 'It is I. Behold my hands and my feet' (Luke 24:39). Jesus' feet were offered in evidence of his risen victory. Uncover the feet of your redeemer! He is risen! He is alive! There is no salvation without a vision of Jesus. And there is no rest for the soul of a sinner until he comes face to face with the risen Saviour, who says 'Behold my hands and feet—a spirit does not have flesh and bones as you see me have' (Luke 24:39). The resurrection is the seal on his saving work, the basis of the hope he gives, and the assurance of the salvation he imparts. It was for this reason that he said in the Old Testament 'I will make the place of my feet glorious' (Isaiah 60:13).

Then, thirdly, Naomi said, *'Lie down and wait.'* That is the language of absolute humility, of absolute subjection. Naomi says to Ruth, 'Wait there at the feet of Boaz.' There were things Ruth had to do—nobody could go to the threshing-floor for her. She had to go there herself. But Naomi was absolutely confident that once there, Boaz would tell her what to do (3:4). It was precisely because Boaz alone could effect the redemption that Ruth needed to make use of this opportunity and go to the threshing-floor of Boaz that very night. This was the accepted time; this was Ruth's day of grace.

It is absolutely fundamental that if we are going to find rest for our soul, we can only find it by shaking off self and lying down at the feet of Jesus Christ. And there is an urgency about the Gospel which means that we dare not delay dealing with this great issue. For Ruth, there was only one redeemer and she had to see him that very night. For us too, there is only one Saviour—and we must go to him immediately. It is one thing to know that he is there—but it is something else to put faith in exercise and go to him, and deal with him person to person.

So Ruth did as she was counselled, and at midnight she uncovered the feet of Boaz. Perhaps the exposure of his feet to the cold stirred him; at any rate, he woke and saw that a woman lay there. It was at that point that Boaz asked Ruth 'Who are you?' I don't think that Boaz failed to recognise her; I think he asked her to identify herself in order to uncover the reasons that led her here at this point in time. What is so troubling her that it has brought her here at midnight when the rest are sleeping? When Ruth is asked 'Who are you?' Boaz is really saying, 'What is it that's leading you here?'

Well, what was it that was leading her there? Why did she come to follow these directives that Naomi had given her and these signposts that had pointed her to Boaz? Well, she came with *a sense of great need*. She came because there was nothing else that she could do. To whom else could she go? Boaz alone had the promise of security and of hope and of rest for her soul. There is a redeemer who alone can deal with the fundamental issue of our estrangement from God, who alone is able definitively and finally to take away every spot and every stain and make us into what we cannot make ourselves. She came in great need.

Have we experienced this sense of need that drives sinners to Christ? Without that sense of need, we will never come to Christ. If the world can satisfy us with what it has to offer, we will sense no need for Christ, and we will not come to him; but every sinner who ever came to Christ came in need. The world develops within us a sense of independence, and of self-reliance. It encourages us to say 'I have need of nothing' (cf. Revelation 3:17), but there is a real need, and only Christ can satisfy and meet that great need.

Ruth also came to Boaz with *great boldness*. She is pushing the boundaries of decency to their limit by coming at this hour of the night to Boaz. Some might question her integrity and her motives, but Ruth is restless. The matter needs to be settled. She can't leave it off. She has to deal with it now, and deal with it finally, once for all. That's why she comes so boldly, even in the night's silent watches, to lie at the feet of Boaz.

The Gospel says that there is life for us now; and that it is *now* we must come to the only one who can give us the life we need. Others may question our integrity and motives, but our need ought to fuel our boldness. The immediacy of the issue ought to remove anything that would tempt us to postpone settling matters between us and God. So Ruth came, in great need, with great boldness, to the right person, at the right time, and in the right place. She came to the threshing-floor of Boaz.

Ruth came with the right petition

What is Ruth's request? There is one thing she asks: 'Spread your robe over me and make me yours.' It is the same image that God uses in Ezekiel 16:8, where God pictures his church as a child left to die by the roadside. God said, 'I came along in a time of love, and I spread my robe over you, and I made you mine'. That is what Boaz does. There is an interesting wordplay between the Hebrew word for the corner of Boaz's garment in 3:4 and the word meaning 'wing' in 2:12. There, Boaz had blessed the Lord that Ruth had come to rest under the shelter and shadow of Jehovah's wings. That is to be realised when Boaz's garment comes to cover Ruth as a symbol of betrothal and marriage. As one commentator puts it, 'this association assumes a theological connection between the two: Boaz's covering of Ruth … implements Yahweh's [Jehovah's] protective covering of her'. Security will come through redemption, and redemption will be made good to Ruth through marriage.

Ruth is given a guarantee: the robe of her redeemer covers her, and it is still the case that a sinner requires nothing more, and can do with nothing less, than the covering of the robe of the redeemer at the feet of Jesus Christ. So in the morning, Ruth comes back to Naomi, who asks the same question, 'Who are you?' It's almost as if she has gone through a total transformation. Matters have been brought to a head. The promise of rest has been given. Ruth will not be the same again. No sinner ever came to Jesus without being transformed as a result. So Naomi asks, 'Who are you?' And Ruth reveals to Naomi the six measures of barley which Boaz gave her. Naomi says, 'He will do the thing'. These measures of barley were a pledge, folded in the veil of Ruth, that Boaz would fulfil the promise he made at the threshing-floor in that midnight meeting.

Those who have found the Lord, who have entrusted the care of their soul to Christ, know what it is to have tokens of his love and assurances of his saving grace folded away in the depth of their heart. When the devil comes saying that our conversion was a sham and that we cannot be genuine Christians at all, let us remember the promises God made to us. Let our mind dwell on what Christ has given us from his word to assure us of his promise. He has covered us with his robe and brought us into a bond of union with himself; as a result, folded away in our soul are these pledges of his love and grace.

There was, however, a difficulty—the fact that there was an unnamed relative who was closer in blood tie than Boaz. But Naomi knows that Boaz will settle the matter. It is interesting that the chapter opens and closes with Naomi speaking. Naomi has become the guide of Ruth. She said to Ruth at the outset 'Shall I not find security for you…?' but she closes the chapter saying 'He will settle the matter today'. Ruth needs rest and security, but the focus of the chapter moves from what Naomi wants to do (verse 1) to what Boaz will certainly do (verse 18). The focus, as in all good preaching, moves from preacher to redeemer. Indeed, the chapter could end on no greater note than this—'he will settle the matter today'. And if that was true of the redeemer in the fields of Bethlehem long ago, how much more is it true of the child of Bethlehem who is the redeemer of God's people. Jesus will settle the matter for all those who trust him, whatever problems and difficulties there may be in the way.

The pledge

You are witnesses today that I have bought everything
which belonged to Elimelech and everything which
belonged to Chilion and Mahlon from the hand of
Naomi. And, more importantly, Ruth the Moabitess, the
wife of Mahlon, I have bought as my wife in order to
perpetuate the name of the dead over his inheritance, so
that the name of the dead will not be cut off … You are
witnesses today. Ruth 4:9–10

In Chapter Three, as we noted, Ruth received the promise and pledge
from Boaz that he would undertake all the duties of a kinsman-
redeemer on her behalf. The threshing-floor in Scripture is the place
where great moments occur and things of great weight and destiny are
transacted. For Ruth the threshing-floor of Boaz becomes the place where
she receives an undertaking from Boaz in whose fields she has gleaned, that
he will provide security for her. And she leaves the threshing-floor with six
measures of barley as his pledge to her.

The closing chapter of Ruth brings us to the climactic moment of the
story, to the culmination of the work of redemption. Ruth came to Boaz
looking to the future, anticipating that Boaz would undertake to redeem
her. We come to Jesus Christ trusting that he will redeem us, only because
he has already paid the price of redemption for us in his death at the cross of
Calvary. Christ has done that work, and has completed that work. All that
is necessary for the redemption of the church has been fulfilled by Jesus
Christ. Here, in the heart of the Old Testament, that great redemptive work
which Christ performed at Calvary is foreshadowed by the action of Boaz.
This is not a spiritualizing of the story of Ruth—it is bringing us to the very
heart of its meaning.

Perhaps a word on Bible interpretation is in order here. There is such a thing as typology—we see the unity of the Bible in the way in which the Old Testament prepares and anticipates the events of the New, and the way in which the New Testament so magnificently and precisely fulfils the Old. There were things which were symbolic to the people of God in the Old Testament; the realities of the covenant of grace within which they enjoyed the blessings of salvation. For Ruth, the action of Boaz as a redemptive agent was a potent symbol of the security Jehovah was providing for her; and what was symbolic for Ruth becomes typological in our reading of the Bible. Boaz is a 'type' of Jesus Christ, and his act of redemption a type of what is done on the cross. What Ruth waited for, we know has been fully accomplished for us in Christ.

If I can go a little further, I would say that Ruth herself is a symbol of the whole of the Old Testament church. Just as she came to her redeemer, and waited for the moment when he would make the transaction guaranteeing her security, so the Old Testament waited for the moment when the great Redeemer would fulfil the work which God required him to do (1 Peter 1:10–12). Just as Ruth had a promise and a pledge from Boaz, so the church in the Old Testament also received God's promise and pledge that a redeemer would come, and in a future moment the great work would be done. The difference between Ruth and us is that we can look back on a work to which Ruth looked forward; and that, in essence, is the difference between the two Testaments which make up our Bible.

Naomi said to Ruth, 'He will finish the thing'. The Gospel says to us that our redeemer has indeed finished the thing. We do not come to Christ *anticipating* that he will redeem; we come to one who has already said 'It is finished'. He has done all that is necessary in order to redeem. Of course, this will be of no benefit to us unless we come to the threshing-floor, to do business with God on the basis of that accomplished redemption. We must come face to face with a redeemer who is equipped and able to save; and in Christ we have such a redeemer, who had transacted all that is necessary for his own church.

The work of the Kinsman-redeemer

You remember that the one thing Ruth wanted was the pledge that Boaz would be her kinsman. The Old Testament sheds light for us on the duties that fell to the kinsman. This person was a near relative to the family. Behind the law regarding the kinsman is the emphasis on the solidarity of the family unit. As you know, in the Old Testament the emphasis on the family unit is very marked. There were some circumstances that could arise in the course of family life in the Old Testament that required the services of a kinsman. If, for example, the blood of a member of the family was shed—if someone was murdered in the family, it was the responsibility of the kinsman to avenge the blood of his relative. It was the kinsman that pursued the murderer. God set apart six cities in Israel to be cities of refuge, to which the slayer of blood could run for refuge and sanctuary. However, the slayer of blood was pursued constantly by the kinsman who was going to avenge the death and the blood of his relative.

There were also instances where a member of the family became so poor that he had to sell himself into slavery. It was the responsibility of the kinsman, if he could, to secure a ransom price that would release that person from his slavery and give him freedom.

The particular duty of the kinsman that is highlighted in the Book of Ruth dealt with property. There was a threefold duty of the kinsman—to respect the *blood* of his relative, the *liberty* of his relative and the *property* of his relative. If for some reason the property or the land was forfeited by the man who owned it and was lost to him because he was poor, it was the duty of the kinsman to try and redeem it until the year of jubilee, every fiftieth year in Israel, when the land was restored to those that originally possessed it.

In the case of Ruth, there was a property issue arising out of the deaths of Elimelech and his sons, one of whom was Ruth's late husband. Since the males of Elimelech's line were dead, here was no-one to keep alive the name or the property of the family, nor was there anyone to maintain the inheritance. Ruth needed someone who would stand in the breach and perform these duties for her.

The great contribution of the Book of Ruth to the theology of the Bible and the revelation of God's salvation, is that it sheds light on us for what it means to secure the services of a redeemer. Ephesians 2 reminds us that we are by nature foreigners from the inheritance of God's people. 'We are aliens,' says the Apostle Paul; we are strangers to God and to the promises of his covenant and to all that he has ever done for his people. By nature we do not belong, we have no rights, no lot, no inheritance. It is because of our poverty and our bankruptcy and our need that we require the work of a redeemer.

Again and again throughout the Bible, God is portrayed as the redeemer of his people. The great psalms of redemption shed light for us on the nature of the work of Christ; there is full redemption with him (Psalm 130:7). This is God's work in Christ, this is what he has accomplished: he and he alone is the redeemer of the church.

It is an interesting thing that the Westminster Shorter Catechism describes him in no other way. It is the word 'redeemer' that the divines used in the Catechism to speak of the glorious work of Jesus Christ, preferring it even to the word 'Saviour'. There can be no salvation unless there is redemption. The redeemer, the only redeemer of God's elect, is the Lord Jesus Christ (see Shorter Catechism Question 21). Ruth needs a redeemer and she finds one in the person of Boaz. We need a redeemer, and we shall find one in the person and work of Jesus Christ.

Let me put it another way. Ruth 4 is going to see Ruth and Boaz marry. Their union will be sealed, and in that closed relationship there is no more doubt and uncertainty; the past is forgotten in the new and higher glory of the marriage union with Boaz. But there can be no wedding unless there is redemption! One of my duties as a minister is to perform marriage ceremonies. People complain, however, of the high cost of getting married. It seems quite absurd in our culture that this most basic, fundamental aspect of our society, that a man and a woman should get married, costs so much financially. How much does a wedding cost? Well—that's the very question that is answered here in Chapter Four of Ruth!

And it is at that level that we see the Gospel shining through this great Book of Ruth. There can be no union with Christ unless there is a redemptive price paid, and unless the redeemer first does his work. Then, and then only can sinners be saved. So let us just note four aspects of this work in Ruth 4: the person, the place, the price and the purpose of this great redemption.

Chapter 10

The Person who Redeems

All Ruth's interests focus now on one single individual. There are many
men in Bethlehem-Judah, many field owners and others coming and going
at the time of harvest but there is only one man who can provide the hope
and the security that Ruth needs. All that will be done by way of
redemption focuses exclusively on that one person. This is a point that has
been emphasised time and again in the course of this great Old Testament
book.

It is also a point that is echoed in the Gospel. Jesus Christ will not share
his position as Redeemer with any other. Every sinner who ever came into
his Kingdom and who ever found salvation and liberty through the Gospel
of the Lord Jesus Christ found it because he became their everything and
their all. The New Testament church was still in its infancy when that
exclusiveness of redemption by Christ was threatened. The letter to the
Galatians was one of the earliest of the New Testament documents, and the
picture Paul paints there is of a situation in which the exclusiveness of
Christ's redeeming work was compromised. False preachers had come into
the Galatian churches and instead of preaching 'Jesus only' they began
preaching 'Jesus plus': a message of Jesus supplemented—by works of the
law, by circumcision, by baptism, by all these other things that were
important in their own right, but which endangered the very gospel itself
when they became supplements to the finished work of Christ at Calvary. It
must be Jesus alone, not another, not Jesus in addition to someone or
something else, not supplemented by anything else, but Jesus only. It was a
lesson the disciples needed to learn on the Mount of Transfiguration.
There, Peter, James and John saw the glory of Jesus as he appeared before
them along with Elijah and Moses. Even after having listened to Jesus
preach, the lesson needed to be reinforced there. A cloud had to come and
take Moses and Elijah away, so that they would be left with no man except
Jesus (Matthew 17:8).

What was it about her redeemer that gave encouragement to Ruth? It was
the guarantee of Naomi that Boaz 'will not rest until the matter is settled
today.' (3:18). It is an interesting thing that there are three different Hebrew
words translated as 'rest' in the Book of Ruth. The first is in Ruth 1:9, when
Naomi said to her daughters-in-law, on the road from Moab, 'The Lord

grant you that you may find *rest*, each of you in the house of her husband.' The word rest there simply means 'a place to stay'. So Orpah went back there, and found a place to stay in Moab. But Ruth could not do that. The rest she wanted and needed was a deeper rest.

At Ruth 3:1, the word 'rest' means 'a place to stand'. It is the word we have in the story of Noah when the dove came back with the leaf because she could find no *rest*, no 'standing place' for her feet. Here at the end of Chapter Three we have another word: 'The man will not be in rest.' This time it means a place of quiet, where there is no more business to be done. It signals that everything has been accomplished; there are no more words to be spoken, no more actions to be performed, everything has been finalised and settled. Ruth found no rest in Moab. Naomi wanted Ruth to find a place of standing in Israel, but that was impossible until Boaz rested from his labour as the redeemer of Ruth.

The great portrait that we have of Christ in the Gospels is of one who would not rest until he had done all that was required for his people and their salvation. God's people needed rest. They needed a place of standing, because for sinners there is no standing in the presence of God. In order to secure a standing for them, their redeemer would not rest. Throughout his life, Jesus is restless to perform the work that has been given him to do. He has been swallowed up with zeal for the house of Jehovah. He set his face like a flint towards Jerusalem and nothing would detract him or distract him from his great purpose. This is how he puts it: 'I have a baptism to be baptized with, and how distressed I am till it is accomplished!' (Luke 12:50). It was the unmistakable emphasis of his ministry: 'he had to go to Jerusalem, and suffer many things from the elders and chief priests and scribes, and be killed, and be raised again the third day' (Matthew 16:21). When Peter said to him, 'Far be it from You, Lord; this shall not happen to you,' Jesus detected in Peter's protestations nothing other than the voice of Satan (Matthew 16:23).

In other words, there is a 'must' about all of Christ's work, a compulsion and a necessity that come to focus at last in the garden of Gethsemane, when the shadows of Calvary flit over the human soul of the Lord Jesus Christ, and there is no avoiding the cup, no distraction from it nor dilution of it. What Christ is given is an unmingled cup to drink. God required that

Jesus Christ experience wrath unmitigated, undiluted, unmixed. He must take it as it is, and he is not going to rest until he secures a ransom price for his church.

Can we not say that the glory of the Gospel is to be found in our restless Redeemer, to whom has been committed the work of redemption on behalf of his people, and who will not rest until he can say, 'It is finished.' The thing is finished, the last word is spoken, the last act performed, the last sacrifice offered, he is the last great High Priest. He has effected the transaction, the thing is over, and only then does he rest in the grave on the Sabbath day. There is an interesting parallel there with the creation narrative, which tells us that God created the world in six days, then rested. In the new act of creating a people for his glory, the Lord Jesus will not rest until the work is completed. When he rose on the first day of the week, he left the old Sabbath in the grave, and he brought a new Sabbath out of the grave for his people in the New Testament. Unlike the church of the Old Testament, we no longer look forward to the Sabbath. In the course of our week, we begin with Sabbath rest. We begin with the sign of resurrection, of work completed, of victory and fulfilment by Christ on our behalf. This one has done all that was necessary for our redemption.

The result of all this is that as far as the salvation of my soul is concerned there is nothing for me to do but come to the blood of Christ. The depth and the profundity of the Gospel are nowhere seen as they are in the simplicity of its invitation. I must come to a perfect redeemer with a finished redemption.

The Place of Redemption

Then we notice *the place* of this redemption. Where did Boaz go in order to redeem? He went to the gate of the city, and he gathered there with the elders of the city, who met there to transact the business of the city. It was at the gate of the city that all the official business was conducted and was contracted.

When Absalom, for example, stole the hearts of the men of Israel, he did it at the gates of the city, where people went in and out. They looked for justice and someone to plead their cause. There was Absalom, waiting there to steal their hearts, at the gate of the city (2 Samuel 15:2). Remember where Jehu slew the sons of Ahab—he did so at the gates of the city

(2 Kings 10:8–11). At the gate of the city was the place where justice and righteousness were upheld and where judgement was transacted. At the gates of the city the claims of God's law were applied to the lives of his people. Psalm 87:2 tells us that more than all the dwellings of Jacob, God delights in the gates of Zion, because he is a just God, and righteousness, justice and truth belong to him. God upholds truth and righteousness in every aspect of his being and activity.

So it was to the gate of the city that Boaz went. He could not redeem Ruth in private. The law would not allow him to do so. It needed to be done in full view of the elders of the city at the city gate. Indeed, there is the greatest contrast drawn for us in this book between the place to which Ruth came, and the place to which Boaz came. The contrast was this: Ruth could come to her redeemer in the quiet of midnight, when no other eye could see; and in the privacy of that meeting, she received from Boaz the pledge and the undertaking of his redemptive work.

But in order to redeem, Boaz had to go in the light of the morning sun to the gate of the city, and present himself to the elders. So it is not insignificant that the writer to the Hebrews says of our great redeemer that 'in order to sanctify the people with his blood, he suffered outside the gate' (Hebrews 13:12). That is where he went. He could not die in private. Eyes had to be on him when he redeemed his church. The eyes of God were upon him when he dealt definitively and finally with the sins of his people, he was before the bar of God in full view of the throne of Heaven. He was in full view of the princes of the earth, who did not know what they were doing; for had they known it they would not have crucified the Lord of glory (1 Corinthians 2:8). The eyes of humankind looked and stared on Jesus, just as the Psalmist had prophesied: 'Upon me they look and they stare' (Psalm 22:17).

Boaz went to the elders of the city in order to do for Ruth what she could not do for herself, and in order to transact business that would secure hope and blessing for her. He goes there as her representative, in her place. If you were to ask Boaz as he makes his way to the entrance of the city, 'Boaz, who are you thinking of?' he would say, 'I am thinking of Ruth.' If you were to ask him as he sits there with the elders transacting business, 'What are you thinking of?' he would say, 'I am thinking of Ruth the Moabitess'. If, in the middle of the transaction, you were able to uncover the heart of Boaz, you would find Ruth.

Let me take you to the cross of Calvary, to the death of Christ, to the finished work of the Saviour. Let me be so bold as to uncover the heart of Christ, as he is crucified between two malefactors. What do I find when I uncover his heart? I see there his church. When I uncover his affections, I see there his bride. When I uncover his purposes, I see there his beloved. He is not thinking of himself. He is thinking of the church that he came to redeem. Powerless to redeem herself; he is there for her. Do you know what it is to have such a saving interest in Christ as to be able to say, 'He loved *me* and that's why he gave *himself*' (Galatians 2:20)?

But there's more. Boaz is going to show favour to Ruth. He is going to *redeem* property, in order to provide security for Ruth, and he can only do it on the grounds of law and of righteousness. Grace, as the New Testament reminds us reigns through righteousness (Romans 5:21), and upholds the demands and the dignity of law. Although it is true that from one angle a righteousness apart from the deeds of the law has now been made manifest (Romans 3:21), the concept of righteousness has no meaning apart from law. So what Paul means is that there is now a righteousness for us that does not depend on law-keeping on our part, since that is the very point at issue—we are sinners and, by definition, law-breakers. If we are to be accepted and declared righteous in the sight of God, we need to rely on the righteousness—the law-keeping—of another.

So Boaz comes to the gates of the city where justice is upheld. Boaz may have been one of the elders himself—he certainly cut a large and important figure in Bethlehem at this time. However, it is only in terms of the law of God that redemption can be effected. In the same way, the Lord Jesus Christ, my redeemer, and Saviour, does not secure my pardon except on the grounds of righteousness. He has upheld God's law, he has made it honourable; and, what is more, every claim that the law of God ever made upon me he has satisfied by upholding all that the law required. He has not simply wiped out all my debts—it would be no Gospel for me to be told that all my debts had simply been overlooked or somehow forgotten. No, the Gospel does not say to me that he has wiped my debts away, the Gospel says to me that he has actually *paid* them and upheld righteousness.

Not only does Boaz show favour to Ruth on the basis of righteousness at the gate of the city, but he does so once and for all. Boaz is here so that Ruth will not need to come here. He is here in order to secure the redemption once, and for all time. Once there has been a *transaction*, there is no possibility of *retraction*. The glory of the Gospel is that what was done once was done once for all. Jesus went to the cross and offered an unrepeated and unrepeatable offering to deal with our sins in the presence of God.

The Price of Redemption

What was the price of redemption? There is no figure set upon the value of the life and property of Elimelech, which would have passed to Chilion and Mahlon, but one thing is clear. There was another man, another relative, who might have redeemed the property and married Ruth. Indeed, he was ready to do so (4:4) until he realised the greater cost—the duty that would fall to him to marry Ruth and raise up a family in the name of Elimelech and his son Mahlon.

This, of course, adds a note of tension into the story. Naomi has advertised her intention to sell the property (4:3), and Boaz has indicated his willingness to buy it, and to perform the duties of a kinsman-redeemer. Behind both of these decisions is the obvious fact that Boaz has fallen in love with Ruth. Suddenly, his plans are jeopardised by the appearance of this contender. There is another option. It is not Boaz's preferred option (nor, by now, is it the reader's), but it is the option set forth in the law.

The story, of course, turns on the information Boaz supplies in 4:5—'the day you buy the field from Naomi, you must also buy it from Ruth, the widow, to perpetuate the name of the dead man and retain the property in the family'. We cannot underemphasise the importance of land in the Old Testament, nor the importance of ownership and inheritance laws. Perhaps the nearer relative only had his eye on the profit that he might accrue from the property, without paying attention to the laws regarding its future possession, and the requirement to retain it within the family of Elimelech. The issue is settled when this player in the drama concedes the redemption right to Boaz. Willing though he may have been to secure possession of the land, he is unable to do it. 'I can't redeem it,' the family redeemer replied, 'because this might endanger my own estate. You redeem the land; I cannot do it' (4:6, NLT). This probably meant that although he could afford the purchase price, to obtain the land would threaten the inheritance of his own children. Supposing he were to marry Ruth and father children in the name of Mahlon, he would only complicate the inheritance and future possession of his own estate. He might gain the land, only for his descendants to lose what they already had.

The statement that he was willing for Boaz to fulfil the duties of redeemer was followed by the strange sandal-ceremony of 4:7–8. There may be a connection with the law of Deuteronomy 25:5–10, where taking off the sandal is referred to. However, the stipulations of that passage seem slightly different to the situation here. One commentator suggests an interesting connection with the uncovering of the feet in 3:4,7, which is now echoed in the removal of the sandal. However, the idea is probably rooted in the fact that ownership was often signified by setting foot on the land, as in the case of Israel in Joshua 1:3, who were told that they would possess those parts of Canaan upon which their feet would tread. To remove one's sandal, therefore, may have represented a forfeiting of possession rights, or, in this case, may have been a statement of non-interest in possession of the land.

In any case, the symbolic gesture was enough to allow Boaz to declare his purchase of the land and his intention to marry Ruth (4:9–10). The deed was done. The obstacles were overcome. The threat was not realised. Love had triumphed.

We must be careful that, in interpreting the symbols of the Old Testament legitimately as typology, we do not go to the opposite extreme of an unwarranted spiritualising or allegorising of the text. It will not do to try to spiritualise the role of the nearer relative, who threatens to spoil the love story. On the other hand, the point is clear: the total act of redemption could not be performed by anyone but Boaz. His contender could not afford all that was required in the redemption price.

There are many contenders out to obtain control of our lives and souls, but every one of them will fall short. There was someone here who declared an interest, but who could not secure redemption. The claim of Boaz, however, was enough, and the price Boaz paid was sufficient when every other price fell short of what was required. He paid what secured the redemption of the property; foreshadowing the great Redeemer of the New Testament, the Son of Man who came not to be ministered unto but to minister and to give his life a ransom (Mark 10:45). Christ uses these images and categories of redemption for interpreting his own mission and life. The rest and security that his people need can only be provided upon payment of a sufficient ransom (cf. Job 33:24). Less than the giving of himself was not sufficient; more than the giving of himself was not required. Christ has paid the redemption price which redeems and releases a soul from sin.

The Purpose of Redemption

So what was the *purpose* of this redemption? Why did Boaz do what he did? He did it in order to buy all that was Elimelech's, to buy all that was Chilion's and Mahlon's and more than this, to purchase Ruth to be his wife. In his public statement of 4:10, there is an echo of times past. Boaz names her Ruth *the Moabitess*. And she is thus named for the last time! Boaz redeems Ruth in order to have her to be his bride, not so that she will remain a Moabitess but so that she will come into the family of the covenant people of God. He redeems in order to marry, and when he marries Ruth, the Moabitess is no more. Ruth is his, and his alone.

Union is effected on the basis of redemption, and a new day dawns. Old things pass away, and all things become new. Love has found a way to wipe out every trace of the past, and to wipe away tears forever. There was a day when Ruth buried her love in Moab. Now love buries away Moab forever, and Ruth is brought into the covenant bond through her marriage to Boaz. She becomes an heiress of God and a joint-heir with Boaz of all the promises God covenanted to his people. She has truly been born again.

The blessing

So Boaz took Ruth, and she became his wife. Then he went to her, and the Lord enabled her to conceive, and she gave birth to a son. The women said to Naomi, 'Praise be to the Lord, who this day has not left you without a kinsman-redeemer. May he become famous throughout Israel … The women living there said 'Naomi has a son'. And they named him Obed. He was the father of Jesse, the father of David. Ruth 4:13–17

In the last chapter, we took special note of what Boaz did in order to secure the redemption of the property that had belonged to Elimelech and to take Ruth to be his own wife. That was a work in which Ruth had no part at all, a work that had to be done for her, and in her place. It represented a purpose of grace that was secured on the ground of law and was upheld by the law. It was an act of special favour that Boaz showed Ruth because of the love that burned in his heart for her. Jesus Christ, the great redeemer of the church, has done his great work for the salvation of his people by rendering complete obedience to the law of God. Now in doing so, all the debts of his people, all the law-breaking, all the sins that they had ever committed have been taken to the cross, to the place of law and judgement. Now God's justice is satisfied and the condemnation is lifted away from the head of God's people. There is no more condemnation to those who are in Christ Jesus.

The young woman who had made her choice in Chapter One to follow Naomi and to join with the people of God, not only became a fellow-labourer in Boaz's fields of harvest, but a fellow-citizen with God's people in Bethlehem, and a fellow-heir of God's promises of covenant blessing. Redemption has become the ground of marriage, and marriage has become the basis for union, consummation and covenant blessing. So we will take note in the remaining verses of Chapter Four of the bride, the birth and the blessing of which these verses speak.

Here Comes the Bride

The elders at the city gate, and all who had witnessed the transaction, invoke the Lord's blessing on Ruth's coming into the house of Boaz. We have noted that the law required that following the death of a husband, it was the right of the kinsman-redeemer, the dead man's brother or close relative, to continue the family name and the family line by undertaking to be a husband for the widow. This included raising up children, to fill the place and perpetuate the name of the man who had gone. That is what Boaz is doing here. Ruth came to Bethlehem as a widow, and as a stranger in a strange land. When Boaz's eye fell on her, his heart went out to her. His fields were open to her, and his riches secured her redemption, which included both the purchase of the inheritance, and the purchase of his bride.

In 4:11 Ruth is compared to Rachel and Leah, the wives of Jacob and matriarchs of the twelve tribes of Israel. 'The Lord make the woman that is come into your house like Rachel and like Leah.' There is a great contrast drawn for us throughout the Book of Ruth between the house that Ruth has left and the house into which she came, between the house that she once had and the house that she now has. All that belonged to her past is now truly past; all things have now become new because Ruth has entered into a new house, into the house of Boaz.

To know the blessing of God's salvation means leaving one home in order to come into another. Psalm 45, which is applied to Christ in Hebrews 1, speaks of the King's bride 'forgetting her people and her father's house' (Psalm 45:10). The King desires to have her. Unless we have experienced this transition from one dwelling to another, this translation, as Colossians 1:13 puts it, from the kingdom of darkness into the kingdom of God's dear Son, we cannot be Christians. A Christian is a person who has discovered the blessing of the old yielding to the new, the old ties dissolved, and a new home and inheritance to be enjoyed.

Perhaps the greatest commentary on these verses is in the great words of

John the Baptist in the New Testament, in John 3:29, as he testified before his audience that he was not the Messiah. This is what John said: '*The bride belongs to the bridegroom. The friend who attends the bridegroom waits and listens for him, and is full of joy when he hears the bridegroom's voice. That joy is mine, and it is now complete*'. John pictures himself as the bridegroom's friend, who shares in the bridegroom's joy when he is united to his bride. Jesus Christ is the great bridegroom of his church, and throughout the Bible—both in the Old Testament (cf. Isaiah 62:4–5) and in the New (cf. Ephesians 5:25–27, Revelation 21:2, 9–10)—the church is the bride whom Christ possesses. He has purchased her and brought her in to his kingdom, he has secured her release from her past way of life, and from the claims that her old life had upon her. He has made everything new, by taking her into his own embrace and making her part of his own life, giving to her a share in his own inheritance, and giving her his own name.

Ruth is no longer the Moabitess; she is now the wife of Boaz. There is a progression in the Book of Ruth: in Chapter One, Ruth is far from Boaz; in Chapter Two she is introduced to him; in Chapter Three she receives a pledge from him; and in Chapter Four she is brought into his home. She moves from being estranged from the redeemer to being his bride. She has come into the town of Boaz, into the fields of Boaz, into the heart of Boaz, and now into the home of Boaz. Here is the Gospel in the Book of Ruth—a Gospel of redeeming love, which brings the stranger in, and which unites those in greatest need to one who can meet that need and make all things new. Covenant blessings become Ruth's because she is brought in to Boaz's home.

What are these blessings that the bride found in the home of Boaz? I think that some of them are brought before us in the words of the witnesses at the gates of the city. 'The Lord make the woman that is come into your house like Rachel and like Leah, which two did build the house of Israel' (Ruth 4:11). There is a contrast here between these two women, Rachel and Leah, and the two women of Ruth 1. Orpah and Ruth went their separate ways, but Rachel and Leah 'built' the house of Israel. They were married to the patriarch Jacob and from them the children of Israel, the tribes of Jacob sprung; through them the blessing of God's salvation was to reach out in to the world and was to be carried along in the stream of human history.

There was, of course, a twist in that love story too. Jacob loved Rachel and worked hard to secure her, but their father, Laban, deceived Jacob (whose very name meant 'the deceiver' and who had previously shown in his conduct that he would get his own way by deception if necessary; see Genesis 27). Jacob had to marry Leah first, and she became the mother of most of his children. Rachel was his true love, however, and her children, Joseph and Benjamin, were especially favoured by Jacob. In God's providence, however, the purposes of his salvation were carried forward. The house of Israel was built on pillars of love, divine love that was woven into human experience, and that was revealed in stories of human love and deception, affection and betrayal, until at last God's true Israel, the people of God, were redeemed by 'the Son of his love'.

It was the prayer of those at the gate that such would be Ruth's experience also: that God's love would be so interwoven with the marriage of Boaz and Ruth that the unfolding story of their home and family would be full of the blessing and grace of God. The love stories of the Bible function at a purely human level here, although their meaning and significance goes much deeper. I think it fails to do justice, for example, to the Song of Solomon, to see it merely as a story of human love. At the same time it is *not less than* a story of human love, and whatever its theological significance might be, the truths which it unfolds have as their point of departure a genuine experience of love, affection and romance. It is the same with the story of Ruth and Boaz. The canonical and theological significance of the Book of Ruth go much deeper than the experience of human love; to see the story of Ruth as merely a love-story is to fail to grasp that significance. Nonetheless, its meaning is rooted in the bonding of two hearts, and its significance is woven into the fabric of that romance and union.

Otherwise we would indeed fail to grasp one of the basic lessons of Ruth—that our relationships, romantic or otherwise, can only be fulfilling as we know the blessing of God upon them. For young people entering into marriage, setting up homes and laying the foundation for family life, there is surely a great moral here. Just as the blessing of God was on the home of Jacob, and now on the home of Boaz, we too need to seek the blessing of God on our homes, families and marriages. The pillars of divine love built the house of Israel. They must be the foundation of our homes and families too.

But there is a greater family, of which our homes and families are faint shadows. The marriage of Christ and the church is archetypal—it is the marriage par excellence, foreshadowed and typified by the marriage of Boaz and Ruth, and brought before us in such clear relief in the New Testament. It is to the consummate marriage of the Book of Revelation that the purposes of God's salvation point. There is a sense in which the angel of Revelation 21:9 speaks for the whole Bible when he says 'Come, I will show you the bride, the Lamb's wife'. That is what the whole of the Scriptures says to us. It shows us the church, the gathered bride of Christ.

The house that is the church is also built on pillars of love, on the foundation of God's love in Christ for his own people, a love that is eternal and unchangeable. 'I have loved you,' God says to his people, 'with an everlasting love' (Jeremiah 31:3). Jacob served willingly and long for Rachel, but the years were just like a few days because of the intensity of his devotion and love for her. What is that in comparison with the love that went to Calvary for the church of Jesus Christ? Christ loved his bride, and he gave himself for his bride. The church of Jesus Christ is built on the pillar of his incomparable love for his own people. And the purposes of his salvation, in and through the covenant seed of his people, in and through each generation of his own witnesses in the world, are the guarantee that Christ's name will endure forever (Psalm 72:17).

That was the purpose of the laws governing marriage and inheritance of property: they all focussed on the perpetuation of the family name. And God's purposes of salvation are also focussed on a name that will abide forever. I have every confidence that the Gospel will be preached to the end of time, and that men will be saved, that there will be a church until the end of time. Even though the church in our experience and in our eyes is often torn and afflicted, and its witness often impoverished and weak, it is not to these phenomena that we must look. Christ's marriage to his bride will ensure that his name will live on! Our confidence is not in men, and not in phenomena, not in things that we can see with our naked eye, but in the unfolding purpose of God's redemption. His name will endure forever, and it will last like the sun, and men will be blessed in him, as the house of Israel was blessed by God through Rachel and Leah and the line of the patriarchs.

So the blessing of God's love, of God's purpose was clear in the family of

Boaz. There was also going to be the blessing of worth and fame : 'May you be great in Ephrathah and famous in Bethlehem' (4:11; NLT). Maybe there were some that didn't know of Boaz and Ruth. But Ruth's name was going to become famous. In the experience of the people of God at the time, she was going to be famous in Bethlehem because she belonged to the household of Boaz. Long after she is gone, and her dust mingles with the dust of the earth, her fame continues because her story is written with the finger of God.

The world is full of men and women who are desperately searching for something by which to be remembered. Their one great aim is to be on everybody's lips, their consuming passion is that men will remember them long after they are gone, that men will remember what they did, and what they said, and the contribution they made in their own field. But everything about us here will pass away, except what God has done and been for us in Christ. Every name that has ever been written in the books of men will vanish, but those that have been written in the Lamb's book of life, written with the finger of God, in his inerrant record of the ages, their name, bound up with the name of their kinsman-redeemer, will live on beyond death in immortal annals. What matters ultimately is not whether men will remember us when we're gone. What matters is whether our name is written in the Lamb's book of life.

The third blessing Ruth will enjoy in the home of Boaz will be the blessing of her descendants. '…may the Lord give you descendants by this young woman who will be like those of our ancestor Perez, the son of Tamar and Judah' (4:12; NLT). This is a reference to an embarrassing, intriguing and important event that is recorded in Genesis 38. The link between Genesis 38 and Ruth is noted in 4:18, where we discover that Boaz was a descendant of Perez. We need, therefore, to take time to work out the significance of this reference.

Genesis 38 is an intriguing passage that interrupts the story of Joseph. Joseph, we learned from Genesis 37, was loved by his father Jacob, and hated by his brothers. They conspired to kill him, but on account of the intervention of Judah, Joseph's life was spared, and he was sold into slavery. It was from the descendants of Judah that the Lord Jesus Christ would be born (cf. Hebrews 7:14). Joseph kept himself pure and maintained his integrity in Egypt, even when he was faced with strong sexual temptation, but Judah, at home in Canaan, had sex with a prostitute, not realising that the woman was actually Tamar, the widow of Judah's eldest son, Er. One purpose of the story is therefore to contrast the two sons of Jacob—Joseph and Judah—and another is to show us why it was that God's judgement came upon the family of Jacob which led them to seek corn in Egypt, from Joseph himself.

There are clear echoes of this passage in the Book of Ruth. When God judged Er for his sin, Judah said to Onan, his brother, that he should observe the law and act as a kinsman to Tamar. He refuses to do so, and God strikes him dead. For a second time, Tamar is left without hope and inheritance. The themes of marriage and widowhood, and the related theme of the kinsman duty, as well as the underlying themes of inheritance and righteousness, undergird both stories, but above all, there is an emphasis on the sovereign purposes of God. For the result of the sinful liason between Judah and Tamar is that Tamar gives birth to twins, Perez and Zerah. When they were about to be born, Zerah's hand appeared first, and a scarlet thread was tied to it. Then Zerah retracted his hand, and Perez was actually the firstborn son of Judah and Tamar. This too echoes the story of the births of Jacob and Esau in Genesis 25:19ff.

The situation of Tamar in Genesis 38, therefore, was very similar to the situation of Ruth. Tamar was a Canaanite who did not belong to the covenant people of God. In the event, however, God overrules the sin of Judah, and Tamar is brought into the covenant line. She is one of only five women mentioned in the genealogy of Christ in Matthew 1 (Rahab, the mother of Boaz, and Ruth, his wife, are two others: see Matthew 1: 3,5). Even though she had sinned, Tamar was fulfilling God's purpose, and Judah had to admit that Tamar was more righteous than he himself was. From their offspring, the result of an illicit union, came Perez, the great-great-great-great-grandfather of Boaz!

It is a principle in the word of God that God's thoughts are higher than ours. His ways are not our ways. He is sovereign in the affairs of men, and is able to over-rule even the most base of our actions for his own glory. The story of the patriarchs, and their ancestors in the pre-patriarchal era, is a story of sovereign, controlling grace. Take the two sons of Adam: Cain and

Abel. Cain was the first-born; he is the symbol of strength and might. He is the one that will inherit—but he's not the man God chooses. God's choice falls on Abel, the second son. Here are the sons of Abraham: Ishmael and Isaac, of whom Ishmael is the first-born. Ordinarily, he is the symbol of the family line, and Abraham's heir, but he is not the one God chooses. God's choice falls on Isaac. Here are the two sons of Isaac: Jacob and Esau. Jacob is the younger; Esau is the one that stands to inherit, but he is not God's choice. God chooses Jacob. Here is Jacob, who has married Rachel and Leah. Jacob's firstborn is Reuben, but the covenant purposes of God focus on Judah, and of the sons of Judah, the covenant line will descend from Perez.

The God of the covenant is a sovereign, deliberating, discriminating God. He acts according to his will among the armies of Heaven and the inhabitants of the earth; none can hold back his hand, or challenge him by asking 'What are you doing?' (Daniel 4:35). The prayer of the people for the house of Boaz is, 'let your house be like the house of Perez'. What kind of house was that? A house marked out, not by men but by God, chosen, not by men, but by God. Its characteristic is that it is a house under the blessing of the sovereign God of the covenant, in which his purposes of grace are executed, and his will for the salvation of men accomplished. In his great evangelistic work, this was Paul's great comfort, assurance and hope: that God had chosen the foolish things of the world to shame the wise; he chose the weak things of the world to shame the strong; he chose the lowly things of the world and the despised things—and the things that are not—to nullify the things that are, so that no-one may boast before him (1 Corinthians 1:27–29). God has chosen the things that men despise in order that he might have all the glory in the work of salvation.

The home of Boaz and Ruth was marked out by God. The midwives marked the hand of Zerah with a scarlet thread, but God had marked out Perez. External symbols are not enough. What lasts, and what matters supremely, is that God, in sovereign, discriminating grace, will mark out our homes and families that we might enjoy the blessings of covenant communion and fellowship. In the destruction of Jericho, as Joshua was about to conquer the city, there was a home marked out by a scarlet cord in the window, placed there as an act of faith that God would fulfil his promise and deliver those who trusted in him. That cord had been placed there by Rahab, the mother of Boaz (Joshua 2:21). That scarlet cord was the symbol of a living faith in a sovereign God. Things did not look too promising, and Rahab was in a minority, but Joshua (interestingly, the name 'Joshua' is the Hebrew equivalent of the name 'Jesus') delivered the house of Rahab (Joshua 6:25).

So unlike Zerah, whose hand had been marked by a scarlet thread, the home of Rahab, marked by the scarlet cord, was saved. In Rahab's case, external sign and inward reality agreed. God's sovereign grace worked faith in Rahab's heart, which moved her to place all her trust and confidence in the God of the covenant.

What a blessing it is when the external symbols of our religion—the sacramental signs of baptism and the Lord's Supper—correspond to a living reality in our hearts! That is the significance of the Sacraments: to show that we are marked out by the grace of the God of the covenant, who alone is able to save. That was the blessing of the lineage of Perez, and it was to be the blessing of Ruth in the household of Boaz too.

Have we come into the household of Jesus Christ? That is where we'll find the blessings of God's redemption, the blessings of God's everlasting love, the blessings of God's salvation. It was the blessing of which Noah prophesied when he said that Japheth would dwell in Shem's tents (Genesis 9:27). The Japhethites would be enlarged and would represent the whole Gentile, non-Jewish world (Genesis 10:5). Yet the sovereign covenant promise was that the Gentiles would enter the tents of Shem, the Semitic race of the Hebrews, through which salvation would come to the world. Christ died for that very reason—that the blessing of Abraham, confined to the Jewish people for the long years of the Old Testament when Satan blinded the eyes of the nations (2 Corinthians 4:4), would come upon the Gentiles through the death of Christ (Galatians 3:14). Satan has been conquered! He cannot deceive the nations any more (Revelation 20:3). The millennium has been inaugurated! The knowledge of the Lord—an integral element of the covenant—now covers the earth, as the waters cover the sea (Isaiah 11:9). Within the Old Testament itself, Ruth, like Tamar, stands as a light in a dark sky, as an example of a Japhethite coming into the tents of Shem, a Gentile woman entering into the blessings of the sovereign covenant of grace.

What a blessing to find our way into the circle and communion of the covenant people of God! At the beginning of the story of Ruth we went out with Elimelech, then we came back with Naomi, and now we've come in with Ruth. The long, cold night of alienation is gone. The day star of hope and resurrection has arisen. There is nothing to compare with being on the inside with the redeemer. As the psalmist David puts it so magnificently in Psalm 118:15, 'there is the melody of joy and health within the dwellings of the righteous'. There is a new song to be sung in the house of Boaz.

Here comes the baby!

I like the King James Version rendering of 4:13: 'Boaz took Ruth and she was his wife, and when he went in unto her the Lord gave her conception and she bare a son'. It underlines for us that the gift of life is the Lord's to give. He gave conception; and as he did so, he continued to unfold his purposes of grace deep inside the body of Ruth. God is a God of moral order, which is seen here; the marriage comes first and then the birth of the son. That is God's design; that is the way he intended that it should be. It was not always so in Bible times, and it is sadly not always so today. However, marriage is God's ordained environment for sexual relations and for the procreation of children.

Soon the home of Boaz is filled, not only with the song of salvation and redemption, but with the song of a child. A son cried, and a new day dawned. At this particular point in the history of God's people in the Old Testament, the hope of Israel focuses on this one child whose name is Obed. The name Obed means a servant. We know little about him, except that he brought great consolation and comfort to Naomi in her old age, and that he was the grandfather of King David. Both Matthew (1:5) and Luke (3:32) remind us of his place in the genealogy of Christ. God's purposes are fulfilled and realised; famines do not thwart them, and accidents of birth do not hinder them. Personal sins do not change their course. God's achievements are equal to his designs.

God's purposes focussed immediately on the son born to Ruth and Boaz, the son given the name of a servant. But ultimately they focussed on Ruth's greater son, who took to himself the name Obed, because he took the form of a servant (Philippians 2:7). The one who is both Son of God and Son of

Man, whose right it is to be served, came to this world, not to exercise his right or stand on his privilege, but to serve (Matthew 20:28). Of him Jehovah can say, 'Behold my servant, whom I uphold; my elect one, in whom my soul delights' (Isaiah 42:1). There it is again—sovereign, discriminating grace, focussing at last upon the one whose whole life was one of service for the salvation and redemption of sinners.

Christ is Boaz and Obed in one; indeed, he is our Boaz because he is all Obed. He redeems because he is a servant. He is God's chosen one, God's elect one; and he at last comes to say 'Not my will, but your will be done' (Matthew 26:39). It is in his service to God that he redeems us. Yes, 'unto us a child is born and a son is given' (Isaiah 9:6), one who will do all that requires to be done for our salvation and for the redemption of God's elect people. He will be the root of Jesse, and in him the Gentiles will trust (Matthew 12:21; Romans 15:12).

Here comes the blessing!

I think that it is one of the most beautiful touches of the Book of Ruth that the women not only bless the Lord because he has provided a kinsman for Naomi, but that they say 'There is a son born to Naomi' (4:17)! Because of Obed, born in the household of Boaz, Naomi enjoyed a special blessing. Many waters had run under her bridge. Nursing Obed brought back her own memories of Elimelech, Mahlon and Chilion, but Ruth, as the women reminded her, was better than seven sons (4:15). I believe that on that day in Bethlehem, when Naomi held Obed in her arms, she did something that she had never done in Moab. She had never nursed a child in Moab. She had buried children in Moab, but she had never nursed a child there. It is here in Bethlehem, in the home of Boaz, within the circle of God's covenant salvation, that Naomi nurses a baby. That's where they sing 'A child is born to Naomi,' in the house of Boaz. Weeping endured for a night, but joy came with the morning (Psalm 30:5).

There is something else too: the same voices that had said in Chapter One, 'Is this Naomi?' now said 'A son is born to Naomi.' Remember when they arrived on the road from Moab and they came to Bethlehem? The whole city was moved. The women noticed that Moab had turned Naomi's hair grey. It had left its scars on her face and in her heart. They didn't even recognise her when she came back saying 'Call me Mara. The Lord has dealt bitterly with me.' But Ruth's son was to be a restorer of Naomi's life. Now she can say 'Call me not Mara. Call me Naomi'. The embittered Mara had gone; the contented Naomi was here to stay.

God has promised to restore the life of his people, to restore in their experience the years that the locusts have eaten (Joel 2:25), the years that sin devoured. God has promised to give back even more besides them. Here was Naomi now, nursing this child in the home of Boaz, living testimony to the faithfullness of the covenant God.

God is going to renew Naomi's youth (Psalm 103:5). She had seen many things, endured many hard experiences, nursed many painful memories. Now her sun was beginning to set, and in old age, when others were fading, she was still bearing fruit (Psalm 92:14). Unlikely as it seemed so long ago, the blessing of God was evident on her life. God promises that though our outward man perishes, the inward man is renewed day by day. So it is with Naomi here, and so it will be with all of God's people. Grace will keep and guard, protect and guide. None will perish that put their trust in him.

In Conclusion

The Book of Ruth ends with a genealogy. We often find in the Old Testament that books *begin* with genealogies, but the story of Ruth explains the genealogy, and this brings us face to face with the purpose of the story. I want to note just one thing about this list of names in 4:18–22: it is both retrospective and prospective. The reference to Perez in 4:18 links the story of Ruth back to the history of the patriarchs, to the family of Jacob, and to the dawn of covenant history in the Book of Genesis. The reference to David in 4:22 links the story forward to the climactic histories of King David, and the greater revelation of the covenant promises to be made to David in 2 Samuel 7. The story of Ruth embraces the whole of Old Testament history—this tremendously rich anticipatory era, in which God was working in the history of the world to prepare the way for the Messiah.

The story of Ruth, in other words, is the Old Testament in miniature. It is the story of sin and its effects as it is the story of grace and its effects; it is an intimation of the blessings of the covenant upon God's chosen people and his faithfullness to them; it tells us of chastisement on disobedience and blessings upon the righteous. Above all, it tells us of the opening of a door by which Gentiles, strangers and foreigners can become fellow-citizens with the saints. It also reminds us that the God who does all of this, focuses his attention on the coming of a Son; for Jesus Christ is the Son of David, the Son of Ruth. Therefore, the Book of Ruth is the perfect complement to the Book of Judges, which tells the story of the era in which Ruth's story was set. Judges may have ended with the statement that there was no king in Israel in those days; but Ruth ends with the name of David, God's chosen king. God's grace abounds in the darkness of man's sin. In these days of rebellion, God has a man after his own heart who can lead those who believe, into victory over sin and death, over doubt and fear. God is at work! He truly is the King!

For further reading

David Atkinson, *The Message of Ruth: The Wings of Refuge*, The Bible Speaks Today, IVP, 1983.

Geoffrey T. Bull, *Love-Song in Harvest: An Interpretation of the Book of Ruth*, Pickering and Inglis, London, 1972.

Stephen Dray, *Judges and Ruth*, Focus on the Bible, Christian Focus Publication, Fearn, 1997

Donald S. Fortner, *Discovering Christ in Ruth: The Kinsman-redeemer*, Evangelical Press, 1999.

C.J. Goslinga, *Joshua, Judges, Ruth*, Bible Student's Commentary, Zondervan, Michigan, 1986

Paul R. House, *Old Testament Theology*, IVP, 1998 (especially Chapter 18)

Robert L. Hubbard jr, *The Book of Ruth*, New International Commentary on the Old Testament, Eerdmans, 1988.

Francine Rivers, *Unshaken*, Tyndale, Illinois, 2001.

Barry G. Webb, *Five Festal Garments: Christian Reflections on The Song of Songs, Ruth, Lamentations, Ecclesiastes and Esther*, New Studies in Biblical Theology, IVP, Illinois, 2000

Warren W. Wiersbe, *Put Your Life Together: Studies in the Book of Ruth*, Victor Books, 1985

Warren W. Wiersbe, *Be Committed: Ruth and Esther*, Scripture Press, 1992

Also from Day One

From despair to hope

Insights into the book of Job

PETER WILLIAMS

224 PAGES

£7.99

1 903087 29 5

A uthor Peter Williams accepts that Job was a historical figure who faced up to real problems about his own suffering, about God's Justice and Government, and about the malignancy of evil in the world. Job is probably one of the world's oldest books and certainly not the easiest to understand, but it conveys some very powerful lessons for today. The author believes that we would greatly benefit by learning from this great man something of the meaning of victory over personal affliction, and the triumph of true faith in Almighty God.

REFERENCE: FDH

Why Lord?

The Book of Job for today

GARY BENFOLD

152 PAGES

£5.99

0 902548 76 X

B enfold skilfully guides us through the book's main themes with brilliant summaries and teaching from elsewhere in Scripture. Concrete examples and varied illustrations drive the lessons home.

REFERENCE: WHY

'Gary Benfold has made the book of Job light reading while maintaining its deep truth'
CHRISTIAN BOOKSTORE JOURNAL

The Resurrection

The unopened gift

GERARD CHRISPIN

176 PAGES

£6.99

1 903087 27 9

G erard Chrispin feels that many walk away from the priceless gift of the resurrection—just there for the unwrapping. We can live like paupers although God's untold riches are within reach! Be it in applying Christ's resurrection to our daily lives, or in letting its light illuminate our understanding of related biblical truth, we must be 'resurrection people'. He is convinced that a grasp of its significance can help an unbeliever to life-changing faith, and encourage all who know Christ to serve and worship Him fully.

REFERENCE: RES

'Reading this book gave me a growing awareness that the truth of Jesus' resurrection influences all areas of our daily Christian lives'
JOHN DARGLE, GRAPEVINE